Henry Ward Beecher

Memorial of Henry Ward Beecher

Henry Ward Beecher

Memorial of Henry Ward Beecher

ISBN/EAN: 9783337141677

Printed in Europe, USA, Canada, Australia, Japan

Cover: Foto ©ninafisch / pixelio.de

More available books at **www.hansebooks.com**

MEMORIAL
—— OF ——
HENRY WARD BEECHER.

NEW YORK:
JOHN H. KNIGHT, PUBLISHER.
1887.

Entered according to Act of Congress in the year 1887, by
John H. Knight,
in the Office of the Librarian of Congress at Washington.

PRESS OF
F. W. SONNEBORN,
8 & 10 WARREN ST.,
NEW YORK.

PREFACE.

IT would be impossible, even in a volume ten times this size, to do anything like justice to the remarkable qualities of Henry Ward Beecher. No one feels this more than the compiler, who for twenty years has been one of his most ardent admirers and a constant attendant upon his public ministrations.

Space does not permit much detail, and so only the more prominent scenes in his life are portrayed, as a collection of paragraphs from his public utterances takes up the greater portion of the work. It has been felt that these gems will, better than anything that could be written, illustrate his wide and original range of thought.

The great man has gone, but while perusing these paragraphs the reader may again stand face to face with him and feel the influence of his master mind. The love of humanity which was the controlling force of his life ; the originality of thought for which he was so widely known ; his touching pathos, his quaint and telling humor, his deep insight into human nature, and his almost universal knowledge, are each and all strikingly illustrated in the paragraphs selected. If ever it was true of man it is pre-eminently so of Henry Ward Beecher, that "He being dead yet speaketh."

HENRY WARD BEECHER.
His Father.

NEVER was there a better illustration of the power of hereditary tendencies than that furnished by Henry Ward Beecher. In his well known eccentricities he was a feeble reproduction of his venerable father, who for more than half a century, kept himself and his denomination in hot water by deeds and utterances quite as sensational and bewildering as any recorded of his illustrious son.

Fifty years ago Lyman Beecher ranked among the first of living pulpit orators, and in his own country was without a rival. He was of all men most fervid in illustration, most fertile in graphic delineation, most effective in utterance. Though the last years of his life were spent in Brooklyn, in which city he died twenty years ago, and though he attained to his chief distinction and career of usefulness in Ohio, it was in New England that he was born and reared and that he reached his first national fame. His ancestors were among the earliest people who settled in New England. He could trace his line directly back to a widow, Hannah Beecher, who settled in New Haven in 1638, eighteen years after the landing of the Pilgrims. He was a graduate of Yale College, and he acquired in that institution an unusual reputation for fine speaking. Beyond the section of New England in which he preached his fame at the start spread slowly, and it was not until 1804, when he was nearly thirty years of age, that an opportunity came for him to be heard by the public at large. In that year he preached a sermon on the death of Alexander Hamilton which drew to him the eyes of half the Nation. It was a truly great sermon for so young a man, and when some years later he gave his heart and genius to the temperance cause six of the sermons that he preached touched the high-water marks of his unrivaled eloquence. Many anecdotes are on record of Lyman Beecher's eccentricities. He was a proverbially absent-minded man, and when he had finished preaching the excitement to which his system had been wrought required to be reduced in peculiar ways. He was accustomed at times to let himself down by playing "Auld Lang Syne" on the violin and by vigorous dancing in the parlor when he reached home. He was three times married, and became the father of thirteen children, eleven of whom in 1872 were still living.

HOUSE IN WHICH MR. BEECHER WAS BORN, AT LITCHFIELD, CONN.

His Mother.

Roxana Foote was descended from Andrew Ward, who came to New Haven in the same year with Hannah Beecher, and she was married to Lyman Beecher in 1799. Seven children had already been born to Lyman and Roxana Beecher when, at Litchfield, Conn., on June 24, 1813, was born Henry Ward Beecher. The father's house at Litchfield was a plain but substantial dwelling, characteristic of its State, standing in a broad inclosure upon a wide and grass-grown street and surrounded by tall and spreading elm trees. Litchfield was a mountain town where the Winters were long and severe, and the snowdrifts frequent and of great size. Here were passed twelve years of Henry Ward Beecher's life. Nature with her giant winds, and storms of sleet and ice, gave him a rugged nursing, and the step-mother that came to him in a few years was also severe, though of good intentions and thoroughly devoted to the welfare of Lyman Beecher's children. His own mother survived Henry's birth only three years. She was a woman of the widest range of sympathy, gentle and tender to her children, and of a restful and serene temperament, which no worldly vexations could disturb. Henry's early impression of her was that she was "the law of purity and the law of honor." He was too young to attend her funeral. Mrs. Stowe remembers his golden curls of that day and the little black frock that he wore "as he frolicked like a kitten in the sun, in ignorant joy." When they had told him his mother had been buried in the ground, and that she had gone to heaven, he was found one morning digging with great zeal beneath his sister Catherine's window, being intent, as he said, on going to heaven to find his mother.

Early Education.

His first school days were spent at a small establishment kept by a Widow Kilbourn, where he was taught to recite the alphabet twice a day. He was then taught arithmetic and writing, and disciplined in readings from the Bible and the "Columbian Orator" at the public school, from which, at the age of ten, he was removed to a private school in the town of Bethlehem, near Litchfield, where, however, he was allowed to roam much at will among fields and woods, his writing meanwhile being bad, his spelling worse. He showed great deficiency in verbal memory, was unusually bashful for a boy and this had retarded his progress.

At the age of twelve years his environment was completely changed by the removal of his father to Boston. While in that city he became prone to melancholy, was restless and irritable, and, from reading lives of Nelson and Capt. Cook, acquired an unconquerable desire to go to sea. The restraint of life in the city, surrounded by high walls and confined for his sport to narrow streets, depressed his mind and distracted his feeling, so that in after-years he believed that, had not a change occurred, he would have gone to destruction. His father, well aware of his sea-going ambitions, shrewdly suggested that he first take a course in mathematics and navigation—a proposition to which the young man gladly acceded. He accordingly departed for the Mount Pleasant school at Amherst, where was soon recorded of him good progress in mathematics and greater clearness of utterance. At the end of a year he had entirely given up his former longing for the sea, had united with his father's church in Boston, and aspired to follow his father's footsteps as a minister of the Gospel.

He Enters College.

Aside from the rude teachings of a country school, Henry learned all he knew until he entered Amherst College in 1830, when he was seventeen years old, at home. His father's house was the headquarters of theological disputation, and many a battle was waged across the hospitable board, while the big eyed children listened to that which no one could explain. Modest and retiring in his manner, Henry listened attentively to the teachings of his stepmother, but the one result in those days was to plant the seed of wonder and inquisitiveness, which grew up and bore Marvellous fruit in later days. A brief period in the Boston Latin School prepared Henry Ward for college, and he entered without trouble. The obtainable record of his experience there does not show brilliantly nor compare favorably with that of scores of men who have lived unnoticed and died unsung. In mathematics alone he was proficient, a fact which stands out clearly and strangely when it is remembered that in later life he was a perfect child in figures, and could never keep the simplest account with any degree of accuracy. In public references to these days of education Mr. Beecher often said that he owed his inspiration for manly living to three persons—his dead mother, whose spirit seemed ever near him as a guardian angel; a negro servant who chopped wood and sung hymns in his father's shed, and the professor of mathematics in Amherst College. He did not study hard in college. He much preferred the excitement of debates, the cheer of the river through the meadows, the singing of birds and the outdoor sports in which he was an adept. That he was a natural born orator is unquestioned, but his shyness so thoroughly controlled him that when a student for a brief time in Mount Pleasant, just before he entered college, his teacher was compelled to reason, plead and almost use force with him to induce him to "speak a piece" in the presence of his fellows. Gradually that bashfulness wore away, and when he entered college he brought the reputation of a ready and graceful speaker.

At that early age he had acquired a taste for physical and physiological science. He was fond of reading in a desultory way, and although his habits were not formed and his tastes were crude, he made the acquaintance of classic writers whose sturdy and vigorous English was to him at once an object of admiration and a lesson.

After leaving Amherst College, which he did without any marked honors or reputation—save that of a jolly good fellow, a choice companion and the chief in the debating societies—Beecher entered Lane Seminary, near Cincinnati, Ohio, where his venerated father was president—then the battlefield whereon the Presbyterians of the old and new schools were fighting fiercely. Dr. Lyman Beecher's heart was in the war and he waged it incessantly and with characteristic vigor. That any son of his should be anything but a minister never entered the old gentleman's mind. All his sons were brought up with the knowledge that they were foreordained to be clergymen, and although two of them, Henry and James, had for a time other views of life, they eventually joined hands with the rest.

In the seminary Henry made a deep impression on the faculty and his fellow students by his oratorical excellence. His father was surprised that he took so little interest in the battle of the Presbyterians, and looked with some doubt on the future usefulness of his son. Nevertheless, he was proud of his abilities and did all he could to ground him in the faith of his fathers. This was a difficult task, and caused the old gentleman many an anxious night, for to him the doctrines were firm and steadfast, and any questioning that tended to unsettle them, or any one of them, was heresy a little less than blasphemy.

First Pastorate.

In 1837, when he was twenty-four years of age, Henry Ward Beecher became the pastor of an independent Presbyterian Church in Lawrenceburg, Ind. He had previously met, wooed, won and married Miss Eunice Bullard, a daughter of Rev. Dr. Bullard, a lady slightly older than himself. Miss Bullard was well born and bred, as the children of Presbyterian clergymen generally are. To an unusually acute wit she united physical and emotional power of rare development. Her energetic nature was a needed complement to the careless dreaminess of the young preacher, and in his early life she was the spur and directer of all his affairs. Like his father, too, Henry Ward Beecher was a man of marked domestic habit. He was the father of eight children—Henry Barton, Harriet B. Scoville, William Constantine, Herbert, Arthur Howard, Alfred Bowen, Kate and George.

In the two years of his Lawrenceburg pastorate Mr. Beecher made his mark. As a preacher he was eloquent; as an orthodox teacher he was not over zealous; as a sympathizing pastor he was of average merit only. His meetings were well attended and he made himself felt. His personal magnetism was great, the flush of vigorous health was in his veins, and he stirred up the dry bones of his neighborhood to such a degree that the attention of a wider circle was attracted, and he was called to take charge of a similar church in Indianapolis, the capital of the State.

Early Struggles.

In Indianapolis young Beecher made friends in several new circles. His church was small and his ministrations at first were held in a room in the second story of the Town Academy. As the son of Lyman Beecher he was accorded a courteous welcome, but it was not long ere he was esteemed and followed for his individual merit. Here, too, in a sense he began to live. Hitherto he had been little better than a home missionary, and indeed he was for some time a beneficiary on the books of the Home Missionary Society. His entire income was less than $300 nominally, and part of that was paid in corn, potatoes and other products of the soil. When he needed a house to live in he hauled the logs himself. His neighbors aided him to put it up. The whitewash and paint he attended to himself. The rapidity with which his children followed each other and the malarial condition of the section in which he lived broke down the strong constitution of his faithful wife, and as they were unable to pay a servant threw on him the domestic drudgery. He chopped the wood, drew the water, peeled the potatoes, cooked the food, served it, washed the dishes and cleaned up the house. When sickness necessitated frequent washings of soiled clothes it was he who did the work. Part of the time he did double duty and rode twenty miles through the woods and across the prairies to the log schoolhouse in which service was held, preached, rode back again, cooked the dinner, preached in his own church, returned to nurse his sick wife and attend to the children, got the supper and spent the evening in the prayer meeting. At times he was so poor that an unpaid letter, on which eighteen or twenty cents were due, remained in the post office, with news from the East, uncalled for because he did not have the money with which to pay the postage.

Poverty and Sympathy.

Added to the poverty of his pocket, the incessant drain of his sympathy at home, the continuous necessity of physical toil in the house, the garden and the woodshed, and the preparation of his sermons, was a doubt, an uncertainty in his beliefs. The little cloud small as a man's hand, that frightened him when a boy, made him gloomy when in college and shadowed him in his first charge, now assumed vast proportions. He was all afloat. All that kept him from sinking—humanly speaking—was his own honest expression of doubt. Had he kept it to himself and brooded over it in secret he might have been carried over the falls of infidelity or gone to the fool's refuge—suicide. But Beecher was then as always, open-mouthed. What he felt, thought or knew he told Secretiveness was never fairly developed in his nature. He never could keep a secret. He made friends easily, and the last person with him invariably knew his mind. He was easily deceived, for, although he had constant experience in human strengths and human weaknesses, he was by nature confiding and trustful. Truthful himself, it was next to impossible to persuade him that any one would be false in speech or inference to him. He knew all about wickedness in general, but special cases bothered him. When doubts assailed him instead of taking them to his study he used them as illustrations in the pulpit. If he questioned the possibility of forgiveness of sin he became the example. It was his breast that he beat, his doubt he asserted, his fears he expressed. In picturing the estate of a lost soul the imagery lost nothing of its power by a personal application. Enthusiastic in everything, from the culture of a flower to the worship of his Saviour, Mr. Beecher carried his zealous search for remedies in this state of doubt to the extremity of his passionate nature. Crowds attended his preaching. Waves of religious feeling carried all classes of people before them. The State of Indiana was in an uproar. The Presbyterian churches looked on amazed. Dr. Lyman Beecher thanked God that he had given him such a son, and in the same breath besceched Him to guide him, lest he should fall. The Legislature sat in Indianapolis, and in its train followed the evils that generally accompany the camp followers. Intemperance, gambling and kindred vices were rampant in the place. Everybody knew it. The sores affected the entire body politic. The members of the Legislature knew it as well as the rest, and winked at it like the rest. This seemed to Beecher a fair target. He announced a series of lectures to young men and delivered them in his church. The feeling engendered by them was intense. Those who were hit were indignant. All classes went to hear them, and before they were concluded a revival arose that swept the city.

His Peculiar Gifts.

He was not the ideal parson. He wore no distinctive garb. His face was round and jolly. His eye was full of laughter. His manner was hearty and his interest sincere. It was often said that Beecher could have attained any desired distinction at the bar or in politics. He was importuned to stand as candidate for legislative honors, but invariably refused even to think of it. At this time, when he regarded himself spiritually weak, he was eloquently strong. He preached without notes and talked as if inspired. His prayers were poems. His illustrations were constant and always changing. He kept his people wide awake and made them feel his earnestness. His acting power was marvellous. Those who knew him well will remember that when talking he could with difficulty sit still. He almost invariably rose, and in the excitement of description or argument acted the entire subject as it struck him. Oftentimes in his most solemn moments an illustration or an odd expression would escape him that sent a laugh from pew to pew. Waking suddenly to the incongruity of the scene and the subject, it almost seemed as if the rebuking spirit of his dead mother stood before him, for with a manner that carried the sympathy of the audience he would drift into a channel tender and deep and full of tears, along which the feelings of his people were irresistibly borne. There, as throughout life, the chief topics of his repertory were the love of God and the dignity of man. He rarely preached from the Old Testament. The thunders of Sinai and the flames of hell had no power over him. It would puzzle an expert to find in all his published sermons—and for more than a generation every word he spoke was reported as he spoke it—a sentence of which threats or fears were the dominant spirit. He preached the love of God and the sympathy of Christ first, last and all the time.

He Visits Brooklyn.

In 1847 Henry Ward Beecher was thirty-four years old. Mentally he had become broader and looked over wider fields than when he began to labor. Morally he was as sincere, as truthful and as ingenuous as when he opened his big blue eyes with astonishment at the Bible stories he heard at "Aunt Esther's" knee. Physically he was a picture of vigorous health. He stood about five feet eight inches high. His large, well formed, well developed head sat defiantly on a short, red neck, that grew from a sturdy frame, rampant and lusty in nerve and fibre and blood and muscle. He had no money, owned no real estate. His capital was in his brains, and they needed the culture procurable in the metropolis alone, where libraries and book stores, art galleries and men of thought were to be met at every turn. A career in the East was far from Beecher's thoughts, and yet his sick wife seemed to need a medicament not to be found in the West. Among the many merchants who from time to time returned to their New York homes to report the singular sayings and Pauline preachings of the Western orator was one who lived in Brooklyn and had incidentally learned that two or three members of the Pilgrim Church were contemplating a second Congregational Church in that city. To them he communicated his impressions of the man he had heard in Indianapolis, and advised them to send for him. The step seemed risky, for even then Brooklyn was known as the City of Churches, and men of mark in divers denominations were drawing audiences to their feet.

Among others at that time were Dr. Bethune, of the Dutch Reformed Church; Dr. Constantine Pise, of the Roman Catholic Church; Dr. R. S. Storrs, Jr., of the Congregational Church; Dr. T. L. Cuyler, of the Presbyterian Church, and *facile princeps* Dr. Samuel Hanson Cox, of the First Presbyterian Church, one of the oldest organizations in the country. Obviously to bring an untried man to a place like Brooklyn was venturesome, to say the least. So it was arranged that Mr. Beecher should be invited to come East for the purpose of addressing the Home Missionary Society, which was shortly to celebrate an anniversary, and that then the Brooklyn church should ask him over to fill its pulpit one or more Sundays. The plan worked like a charm. Mrs. Beecher was overjoyed at the prospect of a trip that might benefit her health and enable her to see her Eastern relatives and friends, and Mr. Beecher was more than glad of anything that would relieve the monotony of a sick room and bring him in contact with a side of the world that was as truly Greek to him as—well, as Greek itself. With scanty wardrobe, old-fashioned and rusty at that, the couple started Eastward. The difference in their appearance may be inferred from a remark made by an old lady on the cars. Mr. Beecher had jumped from the train to the platform at one of the stations to get "Ma," as he always called his wife, a sandwich. "Ma" sat gloomy and sad faced, and attracted the attention of the old lady, who approached her and said, sympathizingly, "Cheer up, my dear madam, cheer up. Surely, whatever may be your trial, you have cause for great thankfulness to God, who has given you such a kind and attentive son." That settled Mrs. Beecher for the remainder of the journey, and made her cup of misery more than full. However, though the lady knew it not, she was rapidly nearing the haven in which she was to find a glowing welcome, reinvigoration of mind and body and an anchorage of safety for life.

From the moment in which he opened his lips in the Broadway Tabernacle, his success was assured. In those days "Anniversary Week" was an institution. The great men of the nation spoke from their platforms. The evangelical expeditions against the heathen, intemperance and slavery were organized, equipped and started then and there. Each year the respective advocates returned with their reports. The Tabernacle was always crowded, and some of

PLYMOUTH CHURCH, BROOKLYN, N.Y.

the best thoughts of the churches' best men were uttered in speeches from that pulpit. Henry Ward Beecher, *per se*, was unknown; but his father and his elder brother and sister were known to every one at all familiar with affairs. Consequently, when the sturdy son of Lyman Beecher rose to speak he was greeted by a friendly audience, and soon found himself at home, although his garb was not in accordance with that of his fashionable hearers.

Called to Plymouth Church.

The ground upon which Plymouth Church now stands and which already contained an edifice of worship, was purchased in June, 1846, for $20,000. Henry C. Bowen, Seth B. Hunt, John T. Howard, and David Hale, the first three being members of the Church of the Pilgrims, furnished $9,500, which sum was paid outright, a mortgage being given for the remainder. Possession was given May 16, 1847, which was the Sunday morning on which Mr. Beecher preached his first sermon in the Plymouth pulpit. He was quite innocent of any knowledge that he was ever to become part and parcel of it. His heart was in the West, and he longed to be home again. An invitation was extended to him to remain and preach a few Sundays. That meant $25 a Sunday and a welcome each week in the house of one of the churchmen. Mrs. Beecher's health seemed to improve and her husband reluctantly consented to continue for a while.

On June 13, Plymouth Church was publicly organized, the Rev. Richard S. Storrs preaching the sermon for the occasion. On the following day, by a unanimous vote, Henry Ward Beecher was elected Pastor, his pastorate being begun on Oct. 10 and the public installation taking place on Nov. 11. Those who took part in the installation were the Rev. Drs. Bushnell, Humphrey, Hewitt, Lansing, R. S. Storrs, J. P. Thompson, and Edward Beecher. At the first services on Oct. 10, the church in the morning was about three-quarters full; in the evening it was completely full, and in a short space of time the edifice was found to be inadequate to the constantly increasing congregation. In a year's time it was found necessary to build a new edifice, and in about one year and a half after the arrival of Mr. Beecher the cornerstone of the present structure was laid. In January of the following year (1850) it was opened for worship.

His Work Against Slavery.

Mr. Beecher at once announced his determination to preach in the Plymouth pulpit Christ as an absolute system of doctrine, by which the ways and usages of society should be judged, and further gave notice that he regarded temperance and anti-slavery principles as a part of that gospel. The excitement caused by the fugitive slave law and Webster's 7th of March speech brought him forward into the arena of practical work. From the pulpit he went into the lecture field, and visited various parts of New York and the New England States. In the *Independent* he began his series of powerful articles under the famous star (*) signature, which were widely read, admired, and heeded. Calhoun, then in his last illness, started up as his secretary, was reading one of these articles, entitled "Shall we Compromise," and exclaimed: "Read that again! That fellow understands his subject; he has gone to the bottom of it." Plymouth Church meanwhile grew steadily stronger in membership, and though dependent entirely for support on the sale of seats, Mr. Beecher made it clearly understood that the buying of a seat would make it necessary for the holders to hear the gospel uncompromisingly applied to the practical issues of the time. When Kansas was being settled, he fearlessly took the ground that emigrants should go out well armed, and caused a subscription to be raised in his church to supply every family with a Bible and a rifle.

A Memorable Scene.

About the time Mr. Beecher first began to deliver set lectures out of town for $50 and his expenses, Charles Sumner was knocked on the head in the Senate Chamber by Brooks, of South Carolina. The entire North was fired with indignation, and the solid merchants of New York thought that was going too far. A mass meeting of protest was called in the Tabernacle, and in order to make it significant no one was invited to speak who had ever countenanced the anti-slavery movement. It was entirely in the hands of conservatives. The chief speakers, resolution readers and fuglemen were Daniel D. Lord, John Van Buren and William M. Evarts. The Tabernacle was packed with an earnest, enthusiastic audience, which, in point of numbers and respectability, culture and influence has rarely been surpassed. For some reason Mr. Beecher, who had been advertised to lecture in Philadelphia that evening, was in the city. He had dined with his friend Mr. Howard, and together they went to the Tabernacle to hear the speaking. As the meeting was about to be closed some one in the audience called out "Beecher." The people took up the cry, and "Beecher, Beecher" resounded through the church. Mr. Evarts, evidently annoyed, advanced to the front of the platform and said:—"The programme of the evening is concluded and the meeting will adjourn. (A voice—"Beecher!") Mr. Beecher, I am told, is lecturing in Philadelphia this evening." "No, he isn't," called out one of the reporters; "there he is behind the pillar." The greater part of the audience had risen and prepared to leave. Beecher was recognized and half led, half forced to the platform from which Mr. Evarts and his friends precipitately retired. John Van Buren, with the instinct of a gentleman, advanced, took Mr. Beecher by the hand and led him to the speaker's place. The audience re-seated themselves, but for fully five minutes, the house was in an uproar of enthusiastic greeting. With a wave of his hand Mr. Beecher secured silence and attention. For an hour he delivered the speech of his life. Every eye glistened. Such applause was never given before. The occasion was an inspiration. The opportunity was one he had never had before. But it is doubtful that he thought of either one or the other. He had the scene in the Senate Chamber in his eye. It was the culminating outrage in a series of horrors. He felt it. He foresaw its end. He made that audience feel what he felt and see what he saw, and when he closed he glowed like a furnace, while the people cheered with their throats full of tears. Such scenes occur once in a lifetime. The next day's papers reported Beecher verbatim and gave the others what they could find space for.

The Keynote of the Campaign.

From that time on the printed and spoken utterances of Henry Ward Beecher were taken as the keynote of the great campaign against slavery and its extension into the free Territories of the Northwest. Some of his people objected strenuously to their pastor's course. They thought it lowered the pulpit and brought religion and politics to a common level. Mr. Beecher met their objections good humoredly but seriously. That any man worthy the name could contemplate the slavery of his fellow and seriously defend an institution whose corner stone was the defilement of the image of God seemed to him an abasement of human intelligence. "Tell me," he said, "that you mean to hold on to slavery because it is profitable or because you love power and I will respect at least your truth, but if you attempt to justify your infamy by scriptural quotations or specious arguments about rights I spew you from my friendship." The "silver-gray" merchants who demurred at his constant agitation of this subject and who affected to regard him as a mountebank he bombarded without mercy. They were rich and in positions of influence, therefore, they were the more dangerous and he spared nothing that would convict them of treachery to the Master whose children and servants they professed to be. By his voice and pen, he stirred the depths of the heart of the nation, and although to many it appeared as if pastor and church were monomaniacs, it must be admitted that they stood together in stormy and troublesome times, faithful witnesses to the great truths of human rights and human liberty. Later on, when, as the result of such agitations, discussion broke out into a flame of war, they did not flinch, but gave their sons and daughters, sending them to the field and to the hospital. He kept a vigilant eye upon affairs and was one on whom men in authority leaned for counsel. He had worked hard to elect Abraham Lincoln, and often thanked God that He had raised such a man from the level of the people. As the nation hesitated in its first step the clarion cry of Beecher recalled it to its duty. Later on, when disaster and defeat sent the thrill of dismay through the North, the voice of Beecher warned the people of the danger of neglecting duty and the infamy of desertion. He wrote and spoke and urged and worked without rest. He counselled the President, cheered the troops and encouraged the people. During the war the church was largely instrumental in raising and equipping a regiment known as the First Long Island Regiment, and many of the young men of the church were members of it, Mr. Beecher's eldest son being an officer. To another regiment—the Fourteenth—the church contributed nearly all the men in two companies. Mr. Beecher became in those days editor of the *Independent*, having been for several years one of its contributors, and was thus able to place before the whole country his views on the great questions of the time. He was in constant communication with prominent men at Washington, and was intimate with the Secretary of War, in whose patriotism and efficiency he had great confidence.

In England in War Times.

Incessant and exhausting labors finally undermined Mr. Beecher's strength and his voice began to fail. It was decided that he should go abroad for temporary rest. His health once before had been broken. This was in March, 1849, when he was severely ill and unable to preach between March and September, and in the following June, under a leave of absence he went abroad. Another leave of absence was granted in 1856, but this was not on account of ill-health. Eminent clergymen and others had requested it "in order that he might traverse the country in behalf of the cause of liberty, then felt to be in peril." On going abroad a second time in June, 1863, he had no idea that he was going in behalf of the cause of liberty, and the many entreaties that were made on his arrival for him to speak in England were uniformly declined. He remained in that country but a short time, going thence to Wales, to Paris, Switzerland, Northern Italy, and Germany. He received in Paris the news that Vicksburg had fallen and that the Union Army had won at Gettysburg. Returning to England he was again asked to speak. He again declined, and on the same ground as before, that this was a quarrel which the Americans must fight out, and which could not be talked. Requests were, however, still pressed upon him, and he was at last made to see that he owed a duty to that small but devoted party which had been holding up the Northern cause in England against heavy odds. A series of engagements were accordingly made for him to speak in the chief cities of England and Scotland. His opening address was made in the Free Trade Hall, at Manchester, to an audience of 6000 persons.

When the orator appeared there at once arose so wild a yell, such a storm of hisses and such an outburst of opprobrium, that braver men would have been justified in declining to face them.

Not so Beecher.

He advanced to the front of the platform and benignantly smiled. He was the embodiment of good nature—fat, round and jolly. His bump of humor was erect and took in the situation. Of physical danger—and there was plenty of it—he had no fear. All he wanted was silence and attention. He made friends with the reporters at once. They spoke to him and he to them. Gradually the uproar diminished and he began to speak. It then repeated itself only again to subside. After a little Mr. Beecher suggested the propriety of a little fair play in the matter, and expressed his perfect faith in the desire of every Englishman present to give him at least half the time. That broke the spell. It was useless to fight a man who laughed. It was folly to spend the evening in shouting at a man who was content to wait until his opponent's throat was choked with hoarseness, and they allowed him to proceed. They soon felt the warmth of his nature and yielded to the magnetism of his manner. Before he had spoken an hour he held the audience in his hand. Then came the tug of war. Scattered in the audience were the Confederate agents. They knew Beecher of old. They appreciated his power and feared precisely what had happened. To divert the audience was their evident cue. But how? By disconcerting Beecher! To accomplish this one after another asked him questions. That was his opportunity. Every question was a text. Each interruption was a chance. Repartee and rejoinder flashed from his lips. Wit and eloquence flowed like water. Possessed of all the facts, historical and political, familiar with the social tendencies of slavery, posted about the leaders and alive to the importance of his victory to the cause of his country, Mr. Beecher gave that audience a specimen of zealous patriotism, American eloquence and sledge hammer argument that compelled them to confess judgment and cheer him to the echo.

His Reception at Home.

That he won his oratorical battles in every place he spoke even his enemies declared. Every word he uttered was reported and printed. He displayed himself in all his best array. He made the people listen to his sober arguments, laugh at his wit and weep when he mourned. The man who had hitherto been known as "Ward Beecher, a brother of Mrs. Beecher Stowe," now had his own firm foundation. Social attentions were showered on him and he became the rage, but the same self-respect that had sustained him when he was literally ignored before, now kept him from the abasement of recognizing aught that did not benefit the cause he served. After a series of oratorical triumphs unprecedented in the annals of the British platform this hardy American Ambassador returned to his home and to a welcome which passes description.

It is not too much to say that when Mr. Beecher returned from England he could have claimed any reward in the gift of the government. But he had his reward in the gratitude of the nation and the affectionate demonstrations of fellow citizens. He simply resumed his work in its several lines, and continued the successes of his life. As the war wore on and the question of Presidential candidates came up, he was outspoken of advocacy of Mr. Lincoln's reelection, and in the following campaign did much to secure that end. When finally the war was happily ended and peace declared he was the first to stretch the hand of reconciliation across the bloody chasm, and in a memorable discourse preached the doctrine of brotherly love. The preoccupation of Fort Sumter and the raising of the old flag was made an occasion of national rejoicing, and Mr. Beecher was chosen as the orator of the day. But grave and gay as were the festivities of that hour they paled into insignificance in the presence of a bereavement that sent the nations of the earth in mourning to our national capital. The death of Lincoln stirred the deepest depths of Beecher's nature, and rung from him a tribute of love and esteem and thoughtful appreciation that will be forever embalmed in the literature of the age. Apprehensive of discord at Washington Mr. Beecher was one of the first to declare in favor of universal amnesty and impartial suffrage. He believed Andrew Johnson to be a good man, and when he wrote his famous Cleveland letter to Charles G. Halpine and his associates he evinced more statesmanlike qualities than his critics at the time understood. Friends fell from him in consequence. There were many who could not forgive and forget. They were willing to say "I forgive," but they had suffered too much to pretend to forget. These frowned on Mr. Beecher and accused him of being a time server. At this he laughed as heartily as when the same people charged him with being foolhardy in his anti-slavery campaign. He said he could afford to wait, and he did.

His Literary Work.

Few persons know what an immense amount of literary work Mr. Beecher accomplished. The following is a list of his published works:—

Sermons, ten volumes of 475 pages each.

Sermons, four volumes of 600 pages each.

"A Summer Parish," 240 pages.

MR. BEECHER'S HOUSE AT PEEKSKILL, N. Y.

"Yale Lectures on Preaching," first, second and third series.

"Lectures to Young Men," 506 pages.

"Star Papers," 600 pages.

"Pleasant Talk about Fruits, Flowers and Farming." 498 pages.

"Lecture Room Talks," 384 pages.

"Norwood; or, Village Life in New England." 549 pages.

"The Overture of Angels."

"Eyes and Ears; or, Thoughts as they Occur."

"Freedom and War."

"Royal Truths."

"Views and Experiences of Religious Subjects."

"Life of Jesus the Christ."

All these in addition to his writings on agricultural, political and general subjects, his routine work and special trips for lecturing or speaking. He was always greatly interested in church music, more especially in the form of congregational singing, and one of the first things done by the new pastor from the West, when he took charge of Plymouth Church, was to compile a book of hymns and tunes for the use of his own and sister churches.

The "Life of Jesus."

For obvious reasons Mr. Beecher's "Life of Jesus the Christ" deserves more than a mention in the list of his writings. During many years he had loved, believed in and taught his people concerning Jesus Christ, in whom all the vitality of his faith appeared to centre. To him Christ was everything and he cared to know no more. His brother clergymen and his own people often asked him to explain his views of Christ. He resolved to put himself on record and to write a book that would inspire a deeper interest in the life and sympathies of his Master. Writing himself about it, Mr. Beecher said :—

"I have undertaken to write a life of Jesus the Christ in the hope of inspiring a deeper interest in the noble Personage of whom those matchless histories, the Gospels of Matthew, Mark, Luke and John, are the chief authentic memorials. I have endeavored to present scenes that occurred two thousand years ago as they would appear to modern eyes if the events had taken place in our day. * * * Writing in full sympathy with the Gospels, as authentic historical documents, and with the nature and teachings of the great Personage whom they describe. * * * I have not invented a life of Jesus to suit the critical philosophy of the nineteenth century. The Jesus of the four Evangelists for well nigh two thousand years has exerted a powerful influence upon the heart, the understanding and the imagination of mankind. It is that Jesus, and not a modern substitute, whom I have sought to depict, in His life, His social relations, His disposition, His deeds and doctrines." * * *

In the latter part of 1872, Ford & Co., issued the first volume—first paying Mr. Beecher $10,000 cash for the completed work yet to be written—and it was at once hailed with enthusiasm by eminent men the world around. Dr. Storrs, of the Church of the Pilgrims, Brooklyn, pronounced it to be "the book which the masses of the Christian world have been waiting for." The religious press, without exception, accorded it a respectful welcome, and scholars and the clergy vied with each other in its praise. A well-known English critic said that Beecher's "Life of Christ" would be welcome to Christians, inquirers, skeptics, infidels, teachers, Bible classes, home circles and intelligent readers of every name. That Mr. Beecher put his best work in the first volume was evident to any critical reader, and the publishers gave it a frame worthy of the picture. Agents sold the book faster than it could be furnished, and that Mr. Beecher would make fortune as well as fame was a moral certainty.

On The Summit Of Prosperity.

At this time it would have been impossible to find a man on the face of the earth on whom the sun of fortune shone more brilliantly than on Henry Ward Beecher. He and his always united Church had just celebrated their silver wedding—the 25th anniversary of their coming together—at which none but sunny memories were disclosed. He was honored by the nation. His influence with the government and the people was equal to that of any one. He was in constant demand as a lecturer, and his appearance in popular assemblages was invariably the signal for genuine and welcoming applause. Although not rich he had an enormous income, which he spent freely and generously. His paper, *The Christian Union*, half of which he owned, had attained a phenomenal circulation, and prosperity "lived upon his business." The Rev. Dr. Storrs, in an address delivered on the 10th of October, 1872, paid him, as the representative of the Christian community, a compliment of which any man in Christendom might well be proud. He at great length analyzed the elements of his power, which he classed in the following sequence ;—First, a thoroughly vitalized mind, its creative faculties in full play all the time ; second, immense common sense, a wonderful self-rectifying judgment ; third, a quick and deep sympathy with men; fourth, mental sensibility; fifth, his wonderful animal vigor, his fulness of bodily power, his voice which can whisper and thunder alike; his sympathy with nature and an enthusiasm for Christ which has certainly been the animating power of his ministry. He spoke of him as the foremost preacher in the American pulpit. After continuing in a most eulogistic strain a long time Dr. Storrs, in the presence of an immense and silent congregation, advanced to Mr. Beecher, who arose, and taking him by the hand. said:—

"I am here to-night to give him the right hand of congratulation on the closing of this twenty-fifth year of his ministry, and to say, God be praised for all the work that you have done here. God be praised for the generous gifts which He has showered upon you, and the generous use which you have made of them, here and elsewhere, and everywhere in the land! God give you many happy and glorious years of work and joy still to come in your ministry on earth! May your soul, as the years go on, be whitened more and more in the radiance of God's light and in the sunshine of His love! And, when the end comes—as it will—may the gates of pearl swing inward for your entrance, before the hands of those who have gone up before you and who now wait to welcome you thither! and then may there open to you that vast and bright eternity—all vivid with God's love—in which an instant vision shall be perfect joy, and an immortal labor shall be to you immortal rest!"

"This magnificent concluding passage," said a local paper the next day, "was uttered with an eloquence that defies description. At its conclusion Mr. Beecher, with tears, and trembling from head to foot, advanced, and placing his hand on Dr. Storr's shoulder, kissed him upon the cheek. The congregation sat for a moment breathless and enraptured with this simple and beautiful action. Then there broke from them such a burst of applause as never before was heard in an ecclesiastical edifice. There was not a dry eye in the house."

Under A Cloud.

At the very flood tide of his popularity and fame and at the height of the usefulness of his church, came the supreme trial of his life. Beginning in a series of whispers, rumors and reports went flying about until in 1874 a committee was appointed by the church to investigate the charges which were finally brought against Mr. Beecher by his professed friend, Theodore Tilton.

To these charges, Mr. Beecher, on August 14th, made a positive denial in an elaborate statement before his congregation. Mr. Moulton, a mutual friend, then came into the matter with a story of the most remarkable confessions and letters. The committee appointed by the church acquitted Mr. Beecher and his enemies were vigorously denounced. Mr. Tilton concluded to go into the courts and brought suit against Mr. Beecher for $100,000. The trial on account of the number and prominence of the witnesses, the length of time it occupied, and its enormous expense on both sides, was one of the most remarkable the country has ever witnessed. Thousands of columns of space in the daily papers were taken up with accounts of it. After eight days consultation the jury found that they could not agree, and the great trial ended without that public vindication which millions of hearts hoped for, expected and desired. This great trouble into which he was led by association with pretended friends only intensified the confidence and affection of his church, the members of which stood by him almost to a man; they never doubted him. While opinion was divided, those who knew him best found it most difficult to believe the charges brought against him, and still more difficult to reconcile the manner in which he bore himself, with his guilt. He stood through it all, self-possessed and calm. With an almost superhuman command over himself, he pursued his daily avocations as though nothing had happened, greeted his friends, faced his enemies and waited; waited, as though conscious that whatever the verdict of the present might be he was secure in the vindication of the future.

There is one point in Mr. Beecher's conduct at this time which cannot fail to elevate him in the estimation of millions of his countrymen, and that is, the manner in which he treated his enemies. During the trial and in all the long years since, in the midst of slander, abuse and denunciation, no words of bitterness fell from his lips or pen, he did not, as he well might have done, use his remarkable powers of wit or satire in retaliation for the abuse heaped upon him.

While his counsel did not succeed in establishing Mr. Beecher's innocence in the minds of all the jurymen they satisfied nine out of the twelve of that fact and showed not alone to the jury, but to the world that the man who brought the charges had, though with full knowledge of the state of affairs, kept quiet for years during which he was receiving help from Mr. Beecher and only sought publicity when a demand for money which was little less than blackmail, was refused.

Mrs. Beecher's Heroism.

In all the annals of domestic faithfulness, there cannot be found a more shining example of devotion to a husband than is presented by the story of her married life. It has been her habit always to guard and defend with infinite care and tenderness the name of the great man who so long ago won her girlish heart and started on that journey of life which has involved every form of trial and sorrow, notwithstanding its many successes and delights. At no time and under no circumstances has she ever failed or flinched when the interests of her husband were at stake. If we could know the whole truth it would very likely appear that but for her robust and indomitable faith, her power of encouragement and her gift of smoothing rough places he would have faltered and missed his chance many times when he went boldly and grandly forward or, possibly, but for that assistance, he would have given up his appointed career, thus depriving the world of the greatest preacher of his time. There must have been not a few occasions when he was tempted to choose rest and safety instead of the strife and peril into which he plunged, and we may be sure that his wife's advice was always a potent force on the side of such a conclusion.

The friends of the great man will never forget how like a heroine Mrs. Beecher behaved during her husband's supreme trouble, when that great wave of scandal rolled over him in connection with the Tiltons. Throughout the whole prolonged and humiliating trial, everybody knows, she was constantly present in the court room, attentive but undismayed, pained to the last point of endurance but still erect, steadfast and confident. It was not merely her husband's reputation, we must remember, but her own honor as well, and the highest interest of her children, living and dead, that were threatened with disaster. The tales to which she had to listen were of a kind which few women could have heard and yet stood firm and self-reliant, as she did — a picture of a wife and mother at her best, of womanhood at its proudest and noblest. If she had wavered for an instant, the scales might have turned to the swift and absolute ruin of the man for whom her remarkable devotion pleaded with such persistent and pathetic emphasis. Though she never said a word, she was Mr. Beecher's most valuable witness. He might, perhaps, have survived the terrible ordeal if she had been absent; but certainly the task would have been a much harder one, and there is reason to believe that he was himself convinced that the aid she rendered him was exceedingly fortunate, if not indispensable.

Birthday Celebration.

The celebration of Mr. Beecher's seventieth birthday at the Academy of Music, Brooklyn, June 25, 1883, was a wonderful manifestation of his popularity in the city of his adoption. It was not an ovation from a mere congregation to whom his labors and his eloquence had endeared him, it was a demonstration of a whole city, and showed how fully he had been restored to popular favor and confidence, to the very hearts of those who were best acquainted with him.

From the parquet to the gayly frescoed roof of the building the Academy was packed. Not even at the great political gatherings which this structure has witnessed has the multitude been greater. Men of all classes, all parties and nearly all religious denominations joined in the jubilee.

In Mr. Beecher's address he said:—

"If there is any one thing that is dearer to my heart than another, it is the belief in an immanent God, in all men and in all things, and what vanity it would be for me to stand here and say that the things of which I have been permitted to be a spectator were mine. They are the footsteps of God. This is the progress that long ago has been predicted and of which we have seen but the opening chapters No man is great of himself, no man is great except by that open channel in him through which God can speak or act. And whoever says anything that shall live for the sake of humanity borrows it; it is not his own. Whoever does anything that is worthy of his time and of his nation, it is God that does it. Work out your own salvation, saith God to the individual and the race, with fear and trembling and earnestness, for it is God that worketh in you to will and do all His good pleasure. When I look down, therefore, into the future my hope and my confidence is that religion is leading men on. My trust and my unshaken hope for the future is that God reigns and the whole earth shall see His salvation. I accept, then, in some sort this gathering to-night, not as testimony to me, but as testimony to my Lord and my Saviour."

In June, 1886, at the earnest desire of friends, Mr. Beecher revisited England, and his heart was cheered by a series of welcomes and receptions, the parallel to which no other American ever enjoyed. During this trip his letters to friends at home were cheerful and characteristically descriptive. Now and then he seemed to lapse into his despondent mood, and once wrote, "It would be a delight to close now my work and go to my rest, unless, indeed, it please God that I must keep on a little longer."

Home to Work and Die.

Vacation ended, Mr. Beecher came home to work and death.

The past winter's record discloses an amazing degree of work laid out and work done. He preached twice every Sunday, and virtually every Friday night as well. He wrote a syndicate letter for the press weekly. He performed the perfunctory duties of his great parish—three in one. He married the young; he buried the old. He attended receptions, made after-dinner speeches and visited all places of public and healthful recreation.

And chief of all he determined to take up anew and finish the "Life of Jesus the Christ." Changing largely the active habit of his outdoor life he confined himself to books, to study, to thought and its outworking. His very heart was in his endeavor. He assigned himself a daily "stint." That is, he finished a certain number of pages a day. It was easy and pleasant to do this, but the mental strain was unusual, the physical restraint was unnatural, and the draught on his emotional nature was tremendous.

He anticipated the end. Indeed, his sermons abound with references to the delight of a sudden and painless death, a sleep from which the awakening should be heaven; and now that he is gone, friends look, and not in vain, for such comfort as can be found in the fact that the great American, our foremost orator, the first citizen of his vicinage, died as he had hoped, he would, in the plenitude of power, on the very pinnacle of fame, beloved by a nation and admired by a world.

His Illness and Death.

Mr. Beecher's oft expressed desire that he might die in the harness and not be subject to a long and lingering illness was granted.

Thursday, March 3rd, 1887, was his last day of health and full consciousness on earth. In company with Mrs. Beecher he spent most of the day in New York, returning home in time for supper. Mrs. Beecher afterward remarked " It was the happiest day of my life. I never knew my husband so lively, tender and joyous before or not in a long time. His mind, heart and health were at their best. He overflowed with talk, both humorous and serious."

That night Mr. Beecher dined with the family, played backgammon in the sitting room, waited for a couple that wanted to be married, went out on an errand and returning early retired at once. During the night Mrs. Beecher, whose room adjoined her husband's, was aroused by a sound in his room. She was at his side in a moment and found him suffering from nausea. He soon fell asleep and remained in that condition until four o'clock the following afternoon, when she summoned the family doctor. Efforts were made to arouse him but the great man never fully regained consciousness. The doctor was not alarmed at first, thinking the prolonged slumber was due to biliousness to which Mr. Beecher was subject. When he returned later in thát day, however, he found that his patient had had a stroke of apoplexy. Mrs. Beecher took the hand of her husband in her own and he gave it a long, strong, loving and earnest pressure. It was farewell—He closed his eyes never to open them again—From that hour until the end, которое came three days later, he remained asleep and unconscious. When the end came the whole family stood or knelt around. Not one of them shed a tear or gave expression to a sob—then and there. The supreme self-control was in obedience to Mr. Beecher's often expressed hope and wish that around his bed of release not tears should fall, but the feeling should prevail as of those who think of a soul gone to a crowning.

Universal Mourning.

The mourning for Mr. Beecher in the city of Brooklyn, may be said to have continued throughout the week of his death, and to have been almost universal. It was very impressive

THE NEW YORK
PUBLIC LIBRARY

LENOX AND
FOUNDATIONS

HOUSE IN WHICH MR. BEECHER DIED, BROOKLYN, N. Y.

for its spontaneity and genuineness. The scenes from day to day as the crowds gathered silently in front of the house where he lay dying, or a little later when stores and dwellings, with never a shred of crape in sight, emulated each other in tasteful displays of Mr. Beecher's favorite flowers, so that the streets at intervals became fairy scenes, especially at evening time, will not soon be forgotten, and may never be repeated. And all this and much more was made impressive by the feeling which incited it. It was not formal homage that was being paid, suggested or helped by near friends. Everybody seemed equally interested.

Nor was it Brooklyn alone that mourned, nor the continent of America. The whole civilized world felt his loss and from many a distant clime the cable flashed messages of regret for humanity's loss and words of sympathy for the stricken family.

The homage to the memory of the man was universal. The sympathy for his family as extended as was that influence with which his superb employment of magnificent capacities girdled the globe.

Christendom was presented with the melancholy but heart-relieving occasion to speak its tribute of love to the liberator of theology. Politics was supplied with the period in which it could say Hail and Farewell to the liberator of the slave. Philanthropy could recall the majesty of mind and the magnetism of manner of him to whom palms of pleading were never stretched out in vain. Partisanship grounded arms around the memory of the statesman. Polemics ceased from dispute in the recollection of the passage of the soul of the apostle of the Gospel of Love. Levity sheathed its blade and put it aside, as the genial humorist wended his unhasting course down the valley. The ethical agencies in governments paused to recall the record of the reformer, who had fallen by the way with his harness on. Journalism discharged its endless duties under the solemnizing shadow of the consciousness that one who was mighty with the pen had sent on the proof sheets of his life to be revised by the Hand of Divine Mercy.

His Funeral.

The day of the funeral (Friday) was a Sabbath in the midst of the week. Business was put aside ostensibly by the advice of the Mayor; really, and from bank to bakeshop, because the general sentiment required it.

There was nothing of gloom in the last public tribute of Brooklyn to her greatest son and to the nation's foremost citizen, whose life, full of worthiness and honors, had fallen ripe from the branch of mortality to become immortal. All day long, through the aisles which led to his coffin, passed the ceaseless stream, never pausing; yet night fell and found tens of thousands still ungratified. Five churches were thronged to hear his praises and thank God for such a man, yet not a tithe of those eager to do him reverence could find a foothold; the streets about his resting place teemed all day with patient hundreds awaiting their turn; no building in the world could have contained the myriads gathered in his name. The flag, his great eloquence had helped to defend rippled its glories in the sun ; the doors of the public buildings were closed; the busy hum of commerce was stilled; bell answered bell from the solemn spires; there was the throb of drums in the street, the flaunting of his regiment's colors and the flash of arms, and through the thoroughfare streamed the rich and the poor, men of all creeds and nationalities. The aged, bowed with years, and many troubles, and children with curls tossing and cheeks aflame, mothers and maidens, the strong and the feeble, all pouring in one common stream to cast a last look on the tranquil face of him whose greatness was of deeds wrought for love of them. Orator, teacher and statesman, philosopher and poet, diplomat, journalist—he was these as well as minister of God; he was the comforter of those in sorrow; he was the helper of those who needed; he enlightened the ignorant; he fought for the slave and the oppressed; he defended those who were in danger; he lifted those who were trodden upon; he guided those who had wandered from the right, and his strength became the strength of the weak—he was all men's friend, and all men's thoughts now turned to him.

Over one hundred thousand persons formed in line and passed through Plymonth Church during the day and the composition of the multitude showed how popular the great pastor had been with all classes. Ladies bred in luxury and attired in its trappings stood in line with their less fortunate and poorly clad sisters. Professional men and wealthy merchants strove in an orderly manner with laboring men, and all in turn with former slaves, for a position that would cut short the wait five minutes. All were bent on the same mission and they braved the cold winds aud incidental inconveniences without a murmur. It took hours for the line to move its entire length, but patience reigned. It was not idle curiosity that moved the crowds, for the difficulties encountered would have extinguished that, but a genuine love for the dead. When, late at night, the doors were finally closed, many yet remained who had not succeeded in gaining admission to the church.

The Scene in Plymouth Church.

There were flowers—flowers everywhere—in Plymouth Church. The casket looked only a a mound of blossoms, for its sides and supports were hidden in a swathing band of roses and its top was lost under a white coverlid of lilies of the valley, with just enough green to break the glare of the white mass. The platform was out of sight, and all that could be seen as a background for the coffin were great masses of buds, of bloom, of blossoms—white roses and pink, and lilies by the hundred. Climbing up to the gallery rail, the rich profusion of the florist's art extended, and then seizing the organ front the greenery ran up, with great callas and tiger lilies flecking the green ground until the ornamentation lost itself in an outburst of mingled white and green close under the ceiling at the top of the organ case. Extending away along the sides of the church ran the surplusage of love-sent blossoms.

And this was the victory of death. Flowers, sunlight, music, the pageant of arms, the dip of the nation's colors, the recital of his glorious life and achievements, the voice of ten thousand in thanksgiving and prayer, the gathering of friends and lovers, the clanging of great bells whose tongues tell only of the passing of the great, the stopping of the wheel of busy life, the hush upon the city—these were answers to the boast of the Destroyer, and upon the lips of the mighty dead was a smile of love and of peace to tell all who beheld him that his last slumber had been blessed and was welcome.

During the life-time of the Rev. Henry Ward Beecher there were many notable gatherings in Plymouth Church, there were many impressive scenes, many solemn ceremonies; but never in the history of that distinguished place of worship was there such an assemblage as on the occasion of the public funeral services of the great divine. All creeds, all denominations, all professions and walks in life were there to do honor to the man they all loved and respected while he lived and worked in their midst. The audience included some of the most prominent men in the country, who had made their names both in the ministry and in other pursuits.

A single anecdote related at his funeral illustrates the character of the great man. On the last Sunday evening of his labor in Plymouth Church, he remained a short time after the congregation had retired from it. The organist and one or two others were practicing the hymn,

"I heard the voice of Jesus say,
Come unto me and rest."

Mr. Beecher, doubtless, with that tire that follows a pastor's Sunday work, remained and listened. Two streets urchins were prompted to wander into the building, and one of them was standing perhaps, in the position of the boy whom Raphael has immortalized, gazing up at the organ. The old man, laying his hands on the boy's head, turned his face upward and kissed him, and with his arms about the two, left the scene of his triumph, his trials and his successes, forever. It was a fitting close to a grand life, the old man of genius and fame shielding the little wanderers, great in breasting traditional ways and prejudices, great also in the gesture, so like him, that recognized, as did the Master, that the humblest and the poorest were his brethren, the great preacher led out into the night by the little nameless waifs. And so he passed from the Church of his labor and his triumphs with his arm about the boys, passing on to the City of God, where he hears again the familiar voice of the Master, saying, "Of such is the kingdom of Heaven."

His Memory.

The character of Henry Ward Beecher will survive his presence and be contemporaneous with his memory here. The impetus supplied by his capacities will yield to the impetus bequeathed by his example. That example will work in ever widening circles until time shall be no longer. Men will find it easier hereafter to be patient and trustful and gentle, because of the great heart that never lost courage, kindness or tranquillity, which loved its enemies, which did good to them that persecuted it and which prayed for them who despitefully used it.

The deathless part of him will forever preach from his tomb as a pulpit and from his books as a text the affluent strength and grace of a mind that mastered many knowledges, of a heart that spoke no evil and which, when reviled, reviled not again, and of a nature that was on confidential terms with the aspirations of the race and attuned with the secrets of the powers of the world to come.

To know him was a liberal education. To pass under the spell of his influence was to rise above what was little, sordid, demeaning and perverting and to fellowship with the noblest forces of the mind and heart, projected upon the solution of the problem of life, or upon the interpretation of epochs, or of cycles of history, or employed in the promotion of brotherhood among men and in the realization of the fondness and the fullness of the fatherhood of God.

Neither was he the slave of any sense of consistency. He grew. He advanced from truth to truth as men climb from crag to crag till they stand on the mountain top, above marsh and fen and the miasma or malaria of the lower world, where the air and the soul are close to nature and where God is not far off. As a whole his life was a series of paradoxes in one sense; but in a better sense it was an evolution from high to higher forms and forces and it broke into benediction as his ascending soul resumed its work beyond.

He was not a man of occasion. His career was not punctuated with a few superlative achievements and otherwise made up of a high or low level of uniform effort. He was keyed to concert pitch always. Great utterances came from him, but they were as likely to come in the little prayer meeting, at the social board, in a passing talk on the street or in a casual car or carriage conversation as in temples of worship or in forums of thought.

And he did and said nothing which in part or as a whole was not stamped with his own genius. His slightest observation had the quality of his entire self in it, just as the rose, broken off of the overladen bush, carries wherever it is borne the fragrance which it did not lose by separation from its sisters.

Mr. Beecher was not a man of institutions. He was an institution in himself. The metes and bounds of denominations did not contain him. They chafed him. He was a poet let loose in theology. He was a philosopher who sought truth and regarded formulated doctrines as the skin of truth set up and stuffed. He was a humanitarian on fire to save men by love and not by rote. He was an agitator thundering against the lets and hindrances which systems, as they affected him, built up between God and the soul. He was indignant at those who would stretch the race in a Procrustes bed of creed and rules. He felt that he came not to call the righteous but sinners to repentance. The greater the sin, the greater the need of Divine pity, he thought. He did not condemn men. He sought by study to account for men and then by study to find means to persuade them or even snare them into good intents. In his arsenal were myriad devices of spiritual strategy as well as the guns that woke the thunders of the hills and the conscience of the hearts.

Hundreds of thousands of hearts will do for themselves a life work, as they feel his loss, before the polar and precise estimates of history are begun. His will be a name in chronicle and tradition and memory to conjure with when all who knew him or heard him have followed him into the silences. Blessed are the eyes that have seen him, and blessed are the ears that have listened to him. Blessed are the lives to whom his life has been education, incitement and inspiration.

But to him are silent the sounds of earth. Upon his raptured ear have fallen the beautiful strains of the Choir Invisible. From the topmost achievement of man, a life lived for God and for humanity, he stepped to the skies as the Gates of Pearl swung inward at his approach.

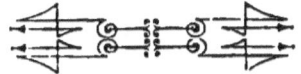

GEMS FROM BEECHER.

THE SPIRIT OF THE DEVIL.

THERE are thousands of men that seem to rejoice in nothing else half so much as iniquity. The moment they hear the servant of the devil asking, "Have you heard the news about A and B?" they say, "What is it? Sit down and tell it to me;" and it is so relishable to reveal, and so exquisite to hear, that A and B have been doing wrong, and have been found out in that wrong, that they fairly gloat over it! This is the very spirit of the devil himself.

ADAM.

WHAT word did Adam ever speak, or what manly thing did he ever perform, before or after his fall, that was thought worthy of a record? He has a name in the Bible and that is all. His name is coupled with one event, and that is all. Besides that his life seems to have been barren, and worth not one word of recognition. Such was the man who is supposed to have been perfect, and from whom the whole race have descended. The race has come up hill every single step from the day of Adam to this!

ADVICE LIKE HAIL-STONES.

ADVICE to unwilling men is like hail-stones on slate roofs; it strikes and rattles and rolls down and does them no good.

THE DRY-GOODS STORE AN ENCYCLOPÆDIA.

THE clerk in the dry-goods store has an encyclopædia on his shelves; if he will trace back the fabrics to the country from whence they came; if he will learn of the soil, the people, and of their history; the processes of machinery by which the fabric was constructed, and a thousand things that suggest themselves to the mind, there is more than he could learn in a lifetime in a store of dry-goods even. If all the knowledge that could be obtained from the dry-goods in Stewart's store were searched out, Appleton's book-store would not hold the books that would have to be written. But if the clerk stands behind the counter all day, and sees in them only so many dry-goods, they are not half so dry as he is.

LIFE A TRADE.

LIFE is a trade, to be learned; a profession, to be gained by education; an art, requiring long drill.

This world is but a primary school; we are learning elements here; and if any man is equal to the emergencies of life under all circumstances, he is out of his sphere.

This is a world where men are *coming* to themselves and not where they have *come* to themselves.

God did not make men perfect. He made them pilgrims after perfection.

CHILDREN.

CHILDREN are God's messengers to us. They are the blossoms of human life. They do not earn anything, and yet how rich we are! How rich are our homes!

A LOWLY HOME.

MANY men are born in a garret or cellar, who fly out of it, as soon as fledged, as fine as anybody. A lowly home has reared many high natures.

WORK, GOD'S BOUNTY.

DO not let any man repine because he has to work from morning till night. Work is God's bounty.

ON CONSCIENCE.

BUT the cultivation of conscience is an art. Conscience is a thing that is learned. No man has much more conscience than he is trained to. So the minister has his conscience; it is according to the training that he has had; and it is thought to be fair for him to hunt a brother minister for heresy, though it would not be fair for him to hunt him for anything else. A lawyer has his conscience. It is sometimes very high, and sometimes it is very low. As an average, it is very good. The doctor has his conscience, and his patients have theirs. Everybody has his conscience, and everybody's conscience acts according to certain lines to which he has been drilled and trained. Right and wrong are to the great mass of men as letters and words. We learn how to spell, and if a man spells wrong, and was taught in that way, nevertheless, it is his way of spelling. And so it is with men's consciences. Now, I aver that mere legislative conscience is genius. Not one man in a million has a sense of what is right and wrong except as the result of education and experience. No man in complex circumstances has a conception of justice and rectitude by a legislative conscience. The great mass of men —teachers and the taught—are obliged to depend upon the revelations of experience to enable them to determine what is right and wrong. They have to set their consciences by the rule of the experiences which they have gone through.

BENEVOLENCE.

BENEVOLENCE has a speaking acquaintance with almost all men's faculties, and that is all. It is intimate and visits in only one or two places in the minds of men.

GOD RAINS NOT BY THE PINT.

I THANK God when I see virtue and true piety existing outside of the church, as well as when I see it existing inside of the church. I recognize the hand of God as being as bountiful, and I recognize His administration as being as broad as are the rains or as is the sunshine. God does not send just as much sunshine as we want for our corn and rye and wheat. It shines on stones and sticks and worms and bugs. It pours its light and heat down upon the mountains and rocks and everywhere. God rains not by the pint nor by the quart, but by the continent Whether things need it or not, He needs to pour out His bounty, that He may relieve Himself of His infinite fullness.

THE COLORED RACE.

I AM bound to say that the black man has proved himself worthy of the trust confided to him. Before emancipation the black man was the most docile laborer that ever the world saw. During the war, and when he knew that liberty was the gage, when he knew that the battle was whether he should or should not be free, although the country for hundreds of miles was stripped bare of able-bodied white men, and when property was at the mercy of the slave, arson or rapine or conspiracy was saved to the country, and no uprising took place. They stood still, conscious of their power, and said: "We will see what God will do for us." Such a history has no parallel. And since they began to vote, after their emancipation, I beg to say that they have voted just as wisely and patriotically as did their late masters before emancipation.

AMERICAN STOCK.

THE best blood of all nations will ultimate by and by in a better race than the primitive and the uncomplex race, mixing new strength and alliances. We have fortified our blood, enriched our blood; we have called the world to be our father and the father of our children and posterity, and there never was a time in the history of this nation when the race stock had in it so much that was worth the study of the physiologist and philanthropist as to-day. We are enriched beyond the power of gratitude. I for one regard all the inconveniences of foreign mixtures, of difference of language, the difference of customs, the difference of religion, the difference in domestic arrangement—I regard all these inconveniences as a trifle; but the augmentation of power, of breadth of manhood, the promise of the future, is past all computation, and there never was, there never began to be in the early day such promise for physical vigor and enriched life as there is to-day upon this continent.

WOMAN'S INFLUENCE.

GOD has placed in woman's hand the rudder of time, for if Eve plucked the apple that Adam might help her to eat it, she has been beforehand with him ever since and steered him. The household that has a bad woman may have an angel for a husband, but he is helpless. The household that has a brute for a husband is safe if the woman be God's own woman. Franklin said that a man is what his wife will let him be. It is more than a proverb, that the children are what the mother makes them. She is the legislator of the household; she is the judge that sits upon the throne of love. All severity comes from love in a mother's hand; she is the educator; she also is the atonement when sins and transgressions have brought children to shame.

AMERICAN WOMEN.

I DECLARE that in the last one hundred years woman, who before had brooded and blossomed in aristocratic circles, has now come to blossom through democratic circles, and is in America to-day undisputed and uncontradicted what before she has been allowed to be only when she had a coronet upon her brow, or some sceptre of power in her hand. Not only is she unveiled, not only is she permitted to show her face where men most do congregate, not only is she a power in the silence of the house, but in the church a teacher. Paul from a thousand years ago may in vain now say, "Let not your women teach in the church." They cannot come there without being teachers and silent letters. They are the books and epistles known and read of all men. They have come to that degree of knowledge, they have come to that breadth of intellect and power, they have learned how to dispose of that primary and highest gift, moral intuition, which God gave to them in excess, cheating man, they have come to such influence and grandeur that never before in any land, certainly never in our own, has womanhood attained such authority and eminence as at the present day. That power which is now latent and applied indirectly, is soon to fill the channels that shall be direct and initial.

ECONOMY USED IN BRAINS.

THE reason, I take it, why so few men are made on a large pattern is that it is not safe to trust a man out in the world with large brains. There is great economy therefore in that direction.

FRETTING.

FRETTING is a perpetual confession of weakness. It says, "I want to, and can't." Fretting is like a little dog pawing and whining at a door, because he can't get in

VALUE OF WORK.

OCCUPATION will go far toward the restraint and cure of all gross and animal lusts. When the salacious devil enters a man, let him put spurs to his industry and work for his life; make the devil pant to keep up with you, and you will run him off his feet, and he will be glad enough to let you alone. Simple food, hard and tiresome work, absorbing occupation and plenty of cold bathing—that will withstand and control a vast amount of evil inclination. Man is to study for these things, and then when you have used all these means, you may pray. But to set yourself to pray, and then go and gorge yourself with stimulating foods and drinks, and not in any way to avail yourself of the proper means, is to mock God and cheat your own soul. Take care of yourself first, and then pray afterward.

MAN NEEDS BREAKING IN.

AS without breaking, the colt is worthless, so man, who is a wild colt indeed, in order to be useful, needs more breaking, more harnessing and more hard work.

PIETY LIKE A CROWN.

THERE are good and perfectional Christians whose piety is like a crown, who, putting it on their heads, say "I am a Christian;" taking it off, say, "I am a Christian; I have only left my Christianity at home." And then they go out into the world, and do all kinds of dirty and mean work; going back again, put on the crown, and say, "I am a Christian again!" If you *are* a Christian, you go to bed a Christian and get up a Christian; you are a Christian at home, in your store, and everywhere.

HE KEPT SUNDAY.

HERE is a man who goes to the judgment, and claims to have been a man of unexceptionable piety. He bears witness that he never violated the Sabbath day; that he never spoke loud or laughed on Sunday; that he never did any secular work on Sunday; that he never blacked his boots, or shaved or cooked on Sunday; that he never rode in the cars or on the boats on Sunday. He was always very scrupulous about what he did on Sunday. On any other day he would not hesitate to take advantage of his fellow-men; he would not hesitate to gouge the poor woman that put his carpet down; he would not hesitate to cheat his customers; but, then, he kept Sunday.

THE GOLD OF PERFORMANCE.

MEN do not take a bank-bill simply because it is a bank-bill. They see whether it is a genuine bill, and whether the bank it is on is able to pay; and if it is a good bill, and on a good bank, they take it on account of the gold there is behind it. And so with professors of religion. When a man knows there is a great deal of bogus religion, he scrutinizes professors to know whether they are counterfeit. He wants to know whether there is the gold of performance behind them.

DANGERS GOD'S WHETSTONES.

THE world would not be fit to live in if there were not dangers in it. Dangers are God's whetstones with which to keep men sharp.

DREAMERS.

THERE are men who live in their imagination. They dream all their life long. On a special impulse they open their eyes, and see things as they are; but the moment the hard, practical necessity which disturbs them has given way, and they are at liberty to do what they love to do best, back they sink into day dreams, and dream up, and down, and out both ways!

A MOTHER'S MEMORY.

IF I were to see a son whose mother's memory was, in his presence, treated with foul scorn and slander, that felt no quickening of his pulse, and that felt no up-rising of soul-indignation, I should almost believe that the mother was all that the slanderer had represented her to be, and that this was the bastard offspring.

EYE AND EAR HUNGER.

PEOPLE should be hungry with the eye and the ear as well as with the mouth. If all a man's necessaries of life go into the porthole of the stomach, it is a bad sign.

POLITENESS.

TRUE politeness can rest only in a kind disposition; though its signs and names may be counterfeited, yet they are never so good as those that are uncounterfeited. The man who is only selfish and indifferent at heart can not be a gentleman. As to those gentlemanly bears that infest society, those bipedal brutes that walk about, flinging their unsavory manners in our midst, they are beneath our notice.

HEALTH—GOOD AND BAD.

IT is not a good thing to have ill-health; but it is a great deal better to have bodily ailments that work out manhood, than good health that works out imbecility.

DON'T JUMP INTO A LIE.

BUT it is said that parents may deceive their children when their inquisitiveness leads them to ask about things which they should not know. If they ask about things which they should not know, then tell them that they should not know. "But," people say, "a child puts a parent in such a disagreeable position sometimes." Well, you hadn't better jump out of it into a lie.

WOULD TO GOD IT MIGHT.

THE fears of men are groundless in regard to the results of scientific investigation. They say, "If you develop this or that doctrine, original sin will go under." Would to God that it might.

DEATH SWEET AS FLOWERS.

DEATH is as sweet as flowers are. It is as blessed as bird-singing in spring. I never hear of the death of any one who is ready to die, that my heart does not sing like a harp. I am sorry for those that are left behind, but not for those who have gone before.

As I grow older and come nearer to death, I look upon it more and more with complacent joy, and out of every longing I hear God say: "O, trusting hungering one, come to me." What the other life will bring I know not, only that I shall awake in God's likeness and see him as He is.

Beat on, then, O heart, and yearn for dying. I have drunk at many a fountain, but thirst came again; I have fed at many a bounteous table, but hunger returned; I have seen many bright and lovely things, but while I gazed their lustre faded.

There is nothing here that can give me rest, but when I behold thee, O God, I shall be satisfied.

MANY DEAD WHO DO NOT KNOW IT.

WHEN a man feels that he has completed his growth in life, he has come to an end, and is dead. There be many men who are dead and do not know it.

THE RACE WORKING UPWARD.

SOMETHING has steadily worked, so that the way of men has grown finer and finer. *Something* has had a power working the way of the human race upward. *I* call it God.

THE BEAUTY OF CHEERFULNESS.

DON"T mope. Be young as long as you live. Laugh a good deal. Frolic every day. A low tone of mind is unhealthy. A lawyer who works ten months in the year and then for two solid months amuses himself, will last twice as long as if he took no recreation. Humor usually tends towards good nature, and everything that tends towards good nature tends towards good grace.

Men have come to think that tears are more sacred than smiles. No! Laughing is as divine as crying. If laughing's a sin, I don't see what the Lord let's so many funny things happen for. Having wit and buoyancy of spirits, let them flash out in services of religion. Don't consider it necessary to rake them up and hide them.

Humor is the atmosphere in which grace most flourishes.

THE PURPOSE OF THE ARK.

IT was not God's plan that the ark should be the refuge of the human race longer than until the deluge had passed away; but if Noah and his descendants had afterward built arks upon the hills and rocks, and attempted to crowd all the people and animals on the earth into them, their folly would not have been greater than is that of those who are attempting to crowd back the gathering forces of the nations into institutions, which were only designed to give them a temporary ferriage while the deluge of an immoral common sense should last.

NARROW MEN.

NO man can be very broad who will build with nothing but that which he quarries from himself. There are men enough who think when they hear themselves echoed that a god spoke.

THE ANGELS' SONG.

THE song of the angels above Bethlehem was caught up on earth, and has never ceased. Yearly its burden swells and mounts heavenward from a vaster host, and to-day millions of hearts are singing, "Glory to God in the highest and on earth peace, good-will toward men."

SINGING FLOWERS.

WHAT a pity flowers can utter no sound! A singing rose, a whispering violet, a murmuring honeysuckle! O, what a rare and exquisite miracle would these be!

A TYPE OF THOUSANDS.

THERE was a man, in the town where I was born, who used to steal all his fire-wood. He would get up on cold nights, and go and take it from his neighbors' wood piles. A computation was made, and it was ascertained that he spent more time, and worked harder, to get his fuel, than he would have been obliged to if he had earned it in an honest way, and at ordinary wages. And this thief was a type of thousands of men who work a great deal harder to please the devil than they would have to work to please God.

AN EXQUISITE LIE.

NOW, suppose I should fall into a controversy with a man, and should adroitly deceive him; and suppose, after having done it, I should come before you, and say, "I told an exquisite lie yesterday. I did not tell it selfishly, however; I told it for a wise purpose, and it inured to the benefit of the truth." How many of you would admire me for owning that I had told a ermissible lie?

IMAGINARY EVILS.

WHY imagine evils that never will happen, and reflect with self-reproach upon things that might have been better done?

RICH BY HONEST INDUSTRY.

I LIKE to see a hard-working honest man, especially if he has had some dirty calling— a butcher, a tallow chandler, or a dealer in fish oil: I like to see such a man, when by dint of honest industry he gets rich, build him a house in the best neighborhood in the place, and build it so that everybody says, "O, what a fine house; it is better taste than we expected." That does me good, makes me fat to the very marrow.

WHO ARE BLESSED.

"HE opened his mouth, and taught them, saying, Blessed are"—oh, who?—"the poor in spirit: theirs is the kingdom of heaven Blessed are they that mourn: they shall be comforted. Blessed are the meek "—what! those spiritless fellows, with white faces, that go about afraid to say their soul is their own?

TRUTH LIKE A BAIT

A TEACHING-TRUTH is like bait on a hook; it must be such a bait as fish will take, and it must be on such a hook as will hold the fish.

DYING GRACE.

GOD won't give us dying grace till it's time to die. What's the use of trying to feel like dying when you're not dying, nor anywhere near it?

SINCERITY.

SINCERITY is a very good thing, but it cannot make grain out of chaff. And that man who thinks that it makes no difference what he believes so long as he is sincere, is a *chaff* farmer.

EXAMPLE.

I REMEMBER a poor colored man who, when I was a boy twelve years old, made a deeper impression on my mind of the goodness of God, than all the sermons to which I had ever listened; and if there was ever a sermon-fed child, I was one. Nothing took so firm a hold upon my higher nature as did the influence of that consistent, praying, psalm-singing, rejoicing colored man, who taught me to work on the farm, and to know that there was something in religion.

RELIGIOUS HYENAS.

AND who does not know that around every church there are just such hyenas whose heads are like to become a fountain of tears at the transgressions of reputable Christians?

TRUE AND FALSE OPINIONS.

OPINIONS are not true simply because they are held to be true in your day.

PERSONAL BITTERNESS.

IF at any time I have seemed to you or to others to run with undue severity upon men, or churches, or orders of men, or institutions, it has never been from any personal bitterness. I do not think I feel personal bitterness toward any man. Nor do I ever feel angry, except when I see one man injuring another. I confess that sometimes, when I see a strong man taking advantage of a weaker one, I do feel an indignation which has a little rancor in it; but I try to pray that down.

WINTER.

COME, bountiful winter, with snows that last till April serves its warmth, and bluebirds warble softly in the cherry trees, and bouncing robins make the morning and evening melodious.

DISHONESTY.

DISHONESTY is an atmosphere. If it comes into one apartment it penetrates all the rest.

PROFANITY AMONG WOMEN.

I WAS going to speak of swearing among women. The only reason why I will not is that I do not wish the young people to know that such a thing ever took place. I have written something upon this subject, which I shall withhold, but I will show it to those who wish to see it, if they will call upon me.

NATURE SPEAKS OF GOD.

I SAY that we are bringing our children up vulgarly, and infidelly, when we teach them to associate God with the Bible, with churches, and with other things that are counted sacred in the world, and do not teach them to associate Him with the works of nature. I think it is much easier to think of the rugged mountain, the brilliant stars, and the effulgent sun, as speaking of God, than to think of dumb churches as speaking of Him.

GOD'S PITY.

I WAS a child of teaching and prayer; I was reared in the household of faith; I knew the Catechism as it was taught; I was instructed in the Scriptures as they were expounded from the pulpit, and read by men; and yet, till after I was twenty-one years old, I groped without the knowledge of God in Christ Jesus. I know not what the tablets of eternity have written down, but I think that when I stand in Zion and before God, the brightest thing which I shall look back upon will be that blessed morning of May, when it pleased God to reveal to my wandering soul the idea that it was His nature to love a man in his sins for the sake of helping him out of them; that he did not do it out of compliment to Christ, or to a law, or a plan of salvation, but from the fullness of his great heart; that he was a Being not made mad by sin, but sorry; that He was not furious with wrath toward the sinner, but pitied him—in short, that He felt toward me as my mother felt toward me, to whose eyes my wrong doing brought tears, who never pressed me so close to her as when I had done wrong, and who would fain, with her yearning love, lift me out of trouble.

SELF-EXAMINATION.

HOW many men have been ruined by self-examination! And yet, tracts and books are published, and sermons are preached, and exhortations are made, without number, urging men to self-examination, as if fantasy must run into folly. Men are set to write journals. I know who invented that trick. The devil invented it! It is a device of his to tempt men.

JUICY IN THEIR INTELLECT.

WHEN a man has certain traits which constitute the leading features of his character, we call those traits his disposition. Thus, there are some men that live in their thoughts. They are dry everywhere except in their intellect; but there they are juicy.

THE IRISH RACE.

THE Irish people stand alone. They are the most mercurial, the most generous, the most distinguished for men of genius, the most admirable creatures that ever troubled the earth.

ENTHUSIASM.

ENTHUSIASM is good to raise men upon, but discipline is the only thing to fight on.

THE ANIMAL NATURE.

THE trouble with men does not generally spring from their reason. It is the animal side of man that fills life with all its trials, and business with all its hindrances.

GOD'S PARABLES.

IN teaching your children, you have to invent little parables, simple stories; you have to go into their play-houses, and make use of the things you find there, likening them to the things you wish to teach. You have to do just what God did in the formation of the Book of Revelation. You are obliged to imagine conditions in the sphere of the child's playthings, his cakes, his tops, his books, his carriages, his knife, or his other trinkets, that shall interpret to him, by his own knowledge, the things you wish to instil into his mind.

COMMON MARTYRS.

THE world will never advance rapidly until we have more martyrs in common things, more witnesses in common places, more men who practice ten thousand little self-denials and duties.

THE PRESENT AGE.

WE of this age have come to the mountain top, as yet we can see only the promise land of the future. Our children shall go over to the land flowing with milk and honey. Great has been the past! The future shall yet be greater.

LIVING PEACEABLY.

WE have no right to be a cause of disturbance by living in that part of our nature which tends to interfere with the happiness or welfare of our fellow-men. No man has a right in any way to annoy others. No man has a right to thrust himself or his affairs forward in such a way that men are compelled to consider him.

DECEPTION.

THE only way in which we can get permission to indulge in equivocations, and evasions, and deceptions, which we refuse to baptize lies, as they ought to be baptized, is by running our moral character down at the heel.

HELL KNOWS THE REST.

HOW many more go on gathering darkness at every step, their feet treading more and more slippery and rough ways, till their character is gone. Their reputation soon follows; with trustworthiness all trust ceases; life becomes a system of dodging expedients; vice becomes crime, and crime becomes destruction; and before half their days are ended, the terrible drama is enacted and the curtain falls, and—Hell knows the rest.

PRIDE.

ONE man ridicules his next-door neighbor on account of his pride; but he would not have known anything about that neighbor's pride if he had not carried his own head so high that he could look over the fence and see how proud he was.

HEADS LIKE GARRETS.

"YES; folks' heads are pretty much like their garrets, where all the rubbish and broken things they've no use for down stairs are stored away."

SHOWER-BATH OF GOLD.

THERE is a vague impression in the minds of men who long for property, that it may reward some rare stroke of skill, that it may turn up at one single more spadeful, just as deluded treasure-seekers, digging at midnight under a glimmering lantern, expect that each next spade-thrust will strike upon an iron chest or crash into an earthen pot full of coin. These men think there is such a thing as dexterity of management, by which wealth may be suddenly obtained, and they think that a hit in the nick of time will bring down a whole shower-bath of gold.

FREEDOM OF THOUGHT.

IF you believe that you have the truth, you are the one above every other who can afford to let every other one think freely.

WORK AND LAZINESS.

IT is not what a man *finds* that does him good, but what he *does*. Active little is better than lazy much.

GOD'S WHISPERS.

I BELIEVE there are whispers of God to the soul. I do not think the Holy Ghost is paraded in the Bible merely to make up the number three in the Godhead.

FALSE IDEAS OF GOD.

IF men have been bitten by this infernal infidelity, if they have come to entertain this false idea, that God is so busy taking care of this world, like a boy driving a hoop through the street, who expects everybody to get out of his way: if men have come to suppose that God is thus busy, so that he cannot take care of the human beings he has created, let them get out of it as soon as possible.

LARGE BUILDINGS.

I THINK the largest buildings in this world, probably, that hold anything, are the Egyptian pyramids, which hold a little king's dust. Next to them, I suppose, some of the largest houses are those which hold the dust of rich men who have not yet hopped out of them.

COURTING.

OH, that men could be kept courting all the days of their life. What a school the school of love is!

ENCOURAGEMENT.

IT is a great deal better for a Christian man to encourage his fellows in well-doing, than to punish them for wrong-thinking.

CALVINISTS, PURITANS AND PRESBYTERIANS.

MEN may talk as much as they please against the Calvinists, and Puritans, and Presbyterians; but you will find that when they want to make an investment they have no objection to Calvinism, or Puritanism, or Presbyterianism. They know that where these systems prevail, where the doctrine of man's obligation to God and men is taught and practiced, there their capital may be safely invested.

PROFESSION AND PRACTICE.

MEN whose life is yet hot with indignation at the oppression which they suffered in their own land, when they come to America are marked, above all others, for arrogance and cruelty to those that are put under them. There is not another nation in this world that has said so much, and said it so eloquently, against dynastic oppressions, as the Irish, and if there is a nation that is meaner than any other in their treatment of their inferiors, it is the Irish. It is their shame. I am sorry that it is so, for the Irish have too many good traits to be disfigured by this one hateful one.

NATURE'S LAWS.

MEN get along very fairly with natural laws everywhere outside of their own stomachs.

IN THEIR OWN JAIL.

BUILD yourselves up first, and then your property. There are many men who build up their fortune first, and build themselves in it, so that when the roof is on they are in their own jail, and cannot get out.

ABUNDANCE NOT HAPPINESS.

A MAN may be a millionaire, and yet be so miserable as to groan all day and curse all night. A man may have all the outside things which the world affords, and yet not be a happy man. One man may have a chest full of excellent tools, and be a bungling workman; while another man may have nothing but a jack-knife, and be a skillful workman.

SECTARIAN SABBATHS.

THE Sabbath is not that conventional, sectarian Sunday which makes a man sigh when he wakes up, and say, "Oh, it is Sunday morning!" and the pleasantest feature of which is the going down of the sun.

IMPURE BOOKS.

BOOKS that poison the imagination and unsettle the moral principles of men are multitudinous, and forever multiplying; subterranean libraries hawked in secret, sold from under the skirts, clandestinely read; books that, like vermin, hide from sight by day in cracks and crevices, and creep out in darkness and at night to suck the very blood of virtue. And this is a business; to write them, to print them, to bind them, to sell them and to hawk and dispense them. There are whole classes of men, and of women—God have mercy on the world!

TRUE HEROISM.

IT is not the general, who knows that he is to stand in the history of the world, that is the more heroic. It is the poor soldier who knows that he shall probably fall in battle without a record, and yet who puts his life in peril for his country.

THE BEST HOUSEHOLD.

THE best household is not that where they have the most hallelujah, but where they have the most order and system and kindness.

PUBLIC EDUCATION.

GIVE the Mayor less. Give the Aldermen less. Reduce salaries everywhere, but increase them in schools.

WOMEN WILL VOTE.

WE permit the lame, the halt, and the blind to go to the ballot-box; we permit the foreigner and the black man, the slave and the freeman to partake of the suffrage; there is but one thing left out, and that is the mother that taught us, and the wife that is thought worthy to walk side by side with us. It is woman that is put lower than the slave, lower than the ignorant foreigner. She is put among the paupers whom the law won't allow to vote, among the insane whom the law won't allow to vote. But the days are numbered in which this can take place, and she too will vote. As in a hundred years suffrage has extended its bonds until it now includes the whole population, in another hundred years everything will vote, unless it be the power of the loom, and locomotive, and watch, and I sometimes think, looking at these machines and their performances, that they too ought to vote.

RATHER TRUST THE PEOPLE.

I WOULD, within the bounds of their knowledge, rather trust the moral judgment and common sense of the millions of the common people than the special knowledge of any hundred of the best trained geniuses that there are in the land. This is not true in respect to those departments of knowledge which the common people have never reached. There is no common sense in astronomy, because there is no common knowledge in astronomy. The same is also true of engineering; but in that whole vast realm of questions which do come down to men's board and bosoms, the moral sense of the great mass of the common people, is more reliable than the judgment of the few. In all those questions there is a common conscience and a common moral sense; and I say that the average moral sense and conscience of the community never were so high as they are to-day—and to-day at such a height in the common people as to be safer in them than in any class in the community.

RELIGIOUS INFLUENCE.

WHEN the Ohio River begins to overflow and overflow, the big Miami bottoms are one sheeted field of water, and where I once lived—in Lawrenceburg, Indiana—I could take a boat and go 25 miles straight across the country, so vast was the volume. Now, suppose a man had taken a skiff and gone out over the fields and plumbed the depth and found only 5 feet of water, and had said "Ah! only five feet of water, and the Ohio had forty feet." Well the Ohio has not shrunk one inch. There are forty feet there and there are 5 feet everywhere else. Religion used to be in the church pretty much and men used to have to measure the church in order to know how deep it was, but there has been rain on the mountains and the moral feeling that exists in the community and in the world has overflowed the bounds of the church, and you can't measure the religious life or the religious impulse of this people unless you measure their philanthropy, their household virtue, and the general good-will that prevails between classes and communities. The church is not less than it has been, it is more than it ever was, but outside of it also there is a vast volume of that which can be registered under no head so well as under that of religious influence.

DOUBLE FOOLS.

THERE are thousands of persons that are doing but little in the present, and nothing for the future, who are always looking back upon the past, and saying, "Oh, if I had done so and so!" or, "Oh, if I had not done so and so!" And thus they make themselves double fools, like the double eagle!

DON'T SWEAR.

A MAN who swears, first damages his own moral sense, then misleads those about him, and then is guilty of cruel impoliteness to those to whom God's name is sweet and sacred.

THE LAW OF HAPPINESS.

THE great law of happiness is the law of outgoing, and not the law of incoming.

STEALING.

MANY a man will steal or *embezzle*, for years, and never once call it by the right name—never! If he happen to say to himself, "I am a thief," he will spring back as if God had spoken to him; it is like poison to him. "Thief!" I don't believe you could make many men steal in that way; but *financiering* is a very different thing. Call it "stealing?" O no; call it an *arrangement*. Call it "thieving?" O no; call it *an unfortunate affair*. Call it "robbery?" O no: it is *an unfortunate mistake*. We talk about bandaging our eyes, but I think men bandage their eyes with their mouths oftener than in any other way.

NOT A REPUTABLE OFFICE.

IN every large church there is a set of men whose business it is to hound their brethren. In many respects they are very good men. So a hangman may be a good man, but his is not a very reputable office. I rather dread these improving people—these folks that go round building everybody up.

THE ANGELS AMUSED.

IT is not particularly agreeable to be rained upon; and yet, what if a man being caught in a shower while on his way to visit a friend, should say, "Oh, what an unfortunate circumstance! Oh my raiment! Oh my skin! A great calamity has befallen me. I am in great trouble. I have met with a serious misfortune!" Why, everybody would laugh at him, except the host; he might refrain from laughing, from politeness; but every child, every servant, and all the rest of the household, would be convulsed with laughter. And I suppose the angels have abundant occupation to laugh at us, when they see what an ado we make about the sprinklings and drenchings we receive in the showers which God sends upon us in the shape of trials and sufferings. God's sons ought to be heroes.

ANXIETY.

"SUPPOSE the last loaf is baked and eaten, and the crumbs are eaten, am I then to trust in God?" What better can you do? If you do not know where the next loaf is to come from, what will you do? Going to be anxious, are you? What good will that do? Is Anxious a baker that he will bring bread?

LET IT BE A CHILD.

MAKE the bridge from the cradle to manhood just as long as you can. Leave your child a child as long as you can—especially if you live in a city. Be not in haste to force your child into premature development by intelligence or by anything else. Let it be a child and not a little ape of a man running about the town.

THUS SAITH THE LORD.

THERE could be no gold if it were not for the pickaxe, the spade, and the stamp; and so there could be no perfect theology if there had been no rude theologies before it. I do not blame them. There was reason for all these successive unfoldings in the church, in the thoughts of religion, that we have had in variety and continuity and that have been crystallized into Christians. "Well, why do you talk so much about them, then?" I reply, that I believe in all these theologies in their time, and for their purpose; but when they have outlived their time and their function, and are brought down to me, and it is insisted that I shall take them because my ancestors did, I won't. The power of any institution is that it digs its own grave. The power of any system is that it makes possible another so much better as that must give way in order to bring a later and better one. I have no objections, therefore, to any form of antiquated theology, only you must not impose it on me, and say in regard to a worn-out thing, "Thus saith the Lord." Thus the Lord did say two thousand years ago, or one thousand years ago, and it was the best that man could have then; but He has not said a word in my time.

FRIENDSHIP.

I WOULD not permit a man to call me his friend who had no other friendship for me but to supply my needs.

The friend himself is the best answer to my wants.

THE DEVIL'S SPAWN.

SATAN loves asceticism. It is the devil's spawn. But joy is a divine element and tends to liberty.

UNKNOWN HEROISM.

THE great virtues of human life are the same in the sight of God, whether achieved in secret and private life, in public spheres, and before men, or upon momentous occasions. Not only are they heroes that are known to be heroes. There is more unknown heroism, a thousand times, than there is visible and recognized heroism in this world. As when we reap the wheat-field with an implement called the *topping-machine*, we go through and cut off all the tops, and leave the straw behind; so it is not yet in the great reaping; for it is not the tall, the well-filled out and the eminent that God is looking upon and ready to sickle. All the way down, among the obscure, the weak, those who are without observation and without influence, there is a sphere of heroism, too.

FLORAL PROPHETS.

EVERY flower, and every tree, and every root, are annual prophets sent to affirm the future and cheer the way.

FEAR AND LOVE.

THERE is nothing that is so convicting of sin as putting over against sinfulness right conduct, the element of the beautiful, the holy, the true. It is not fear which has been the principal instrument of striking conviction into men's hearts. That is not the most powerful and fruitful in producing a sense of sinfulness. The beauty of holiness, the wonder and glory of love, are more convicting of sin, a thousand times, to a generous soul, than the thunders of hell itself. Sinai may smoke; but let Calvary sigh, and say, "Father," and Calvary is the mightier of the two.

DECEMBER.

KNOW, O month of destruction, that in thy constellation is set that Star whose rising is the sign, forevermore, that there is life in death.

EARLY TRAINING.

IF homœopathy be true, a drop of color changes more or less the color of the whole Atlantic Ocean. Of course it is attenuated, and our senses cannot discern it, but it is there. So the things we do for the interior life of a child we lose from sight and forget; but they remain as active forces in association with others, in complexity, and go on acting clear down to the very end of the child's life. It is a dangerous thing, therefore, to infuse malign elements into a child's life; and it is a glorious thing to introduce the elements of love, purity, and truth; for although they may not appear to-day, and may seem to disappear in a score of years, they are latent. A thousand times they come back. In the last years of his life, when he has wrestled with adversity, and the outcome and finality come, it will be found that, after all, the threads that were put in the mother's loom have not broken, and the fabric retains them to the very end.

SOWING AND REAPING.

ONE man sows, and another reaps; but they shall rejoice together. The land of rejoicing is above and beyond. It is there that they meet who were unknown benefactors to each other. There they who were but drops that fell into the river of life, which is the river of love, recognize each other. Those affinities that we feel in their greatest force in the household will have a wider sphere, a more glorious expansion, in the world to come. In the great invisible toward which we are going, we shall find ten thousand vibrating strings which we have made musical, which the whole heavens shall chant, and which the whole earth will hear.

GREAT MEN.

THE men that are great are the men that had no consciousness of it or expectation of it. God made them great—or their mothers; for God through mothers does the best work that is done in the world. When the times and the emergencies came these men were competent for them, and rose to them, and showed that they were great; and after they were dead everybody admitted it.

What a revolution of judgments there will be when men are dead! I do not despair, in some future tract society, to hear some tractarian say, "That great and pious Henry Ward Beecher." There is no telling what a man may come to.

PERFECTION.

THE idea of a perfect man or a perfect woman in this world, is one of the sweetest jests that I ever roll under my tongue.

OUR DUTY TOWARD OTHERS.

YOU have no right to be unconcerned whether men act rightly or wrongly—whether they are good or bad. That spirit which says, "I will take care of my own self, and let other men take care of themselves," is of the devil. The spirit of God is this: "Look not every man on his own things, but every man also on the things of another."

PATIENCE.

I DO not attempt to ripen my apples by throwing stones at them. Oh, that we could be as patient with each other as we are with apple trees.

LYING TRUTHS.

I SAY that a person may so tell the truth as to tell a lie at the same time; as when a man, offering to sell a mocking-bird, and being asked whether it would sing, replied, "Oh! it will delight thee to hear it sing," on the strength of which reply it was purchased. There is no question but that the man who purchased it would have been exceedingly delighted to hear it sing, but he never did.

RELIGIOUS FEELING.

I BELIEVE that no other persons can have such health of body and soul as they who are accustomed to high, fervent, sweet religious feeling.

LIVING MUMMIES.

THERE are many men who coin every drop of manly blood in them to get money; and when they have got it, they are miserable desiccated mummies, only needing the cerements on them to make them complete!

FAMILY PRAYER.

ANY man who has a family round about him, whatever it may cost in the beginning, will do wisely to take up family prayer. As to reading of it from a book, every man must have his own liberty. It is better to read than not to pray; but it is still better to read from your own religious experience than from any other volume. A man who walks with crutches is better than a man who does not walk at all.

CYPHER BOTH WAYS.

CYPHER both ways, not only toward heaven, but also toward hell; and make up your mind what you will do from a comprehensive calculation, and not a partial and flattering one.

THE POWER OF HOME.

THE power of a home shows. It never lets go its hold. A mother has often reeled in a boy by the line of love, and a father's memory has brought many back.

ONE SIDED RECONCILIATION.

WHEN a church was about to be built in a certain town, the people were divided with reference to where it should stand, and the minister had to preach a very strong sermon on the subject. This sermon had the desired effect. It even brought tears to the eyes of the deacons —and it is a good sign when deacons cry. The next morning one deacon called on another, and said to him, "Our minister is right, and we are imperiling the cause of Christ by our dissension, and I have come to tell you that we must compromise; and now, you must give up, for I can't."

THE ORIGIN OF EVIL.

THE origin of evil is a cob that has been gnawed upon for thousands of years, but no one ever got a kernel from it. It is still a cob.

COPYISTS NOT ARTISTS.

COPYISTS are not artists, any more than a dog is an artist because he draws a little baby in a wagon behind him!

A CRACKED FRIENDSHIP.

IF you cut off a branch of a tree, and immediately bandage it, so as not to allow the air to get at the wound, it will grow again; but if you crack a crystal vase, no growing process in creation will repair the damage. It is cracked glass forever and forever. Nothing will take out the crack. Now, although a cracked friendship, like a cracked tumbler, may be cemented, the moment you put it into hot water the bottom will fall out or it will come to pieces!

FRETFUL PEOPLE.

PERSONS that are fretful in youth and in middle age are usually so through old age, and they go croaking to the end of their days, when, reptile-like, they crawl out of life.

THANKSGIVING DAY.

A THANKSGIVING dinner represents everything that has grown in all the summer fit to make glad the heart of man. It is a table piled high with the treasures of the growing year, accepted with rejoicings, as a token of gratitude to God. It is an American day.

OLD SAXON WORDS.

OLD Saxon words are Day of Judgment words; they are like double-edged swords, and cut where they hit. But when we come to speak of evil, we must have Latin, or some soft language. I think it will take two or three languages for us to get along with, soon.

ANGER.

DO not be angry by the day. Be angry when there is a just cause for it, but get over it as speedily as possible. A man could not live and be in a constant blaze of anger. It is only now and then that one can afford to be angry

ON DOING GOOD.

DO not do some good thing on purpose that you may be happy. You must do good for the sake of doing good, and not for the sake of the kicking back of happiness.

GOD'S PLAN.

THEREFORE although I would not speak contemptuously of any form of words that may have become endeared to any man's experience, yet I may say, so far as my own experience is concerned, I utterly abhor such terms as "God's plan," and as the "plan of salvation;" as though there had been endless cypherings, plannings, fixings and arrangements, and at last there was something devised, and God's heart uplifted salvation.

VALUE OF LABOR.

LET parents who hate their offspring rear them to hate labor, and before long they will be stung by every vice, racked by its poison, and damned by its penalty.

INFIRMITY NOT SIN.

MEN are responsible for sin, but not for infirmity. Infirmities are the mistakes which men make on their way to knowledge.

The only sin in this world is voluntary transgression. It is when a man knows what is right and *won't*; when he knows what is wrong and *will*.

GOOD FOR NOTHING MEN.

ALL along the shores of life I see men in middle life lay themselves up; and there they lie shrinking and cracking, good for nothing on sea or on land. Now, if anybody wants to retire, die!

VICE A DELIGHT.

THE same terrible instinct that is in many birds of prey, by which they have a palate for carrion, and scent it afar off, seems to be in the bosoms of a great many men in the world. The first hint of scandal is like the wine of intoxication to them. "How shall the thing be found out?" they say to themselves. "How shall it be opened up? How shall the parties involved be identified and convicted?" And if, when they have found it out, it proves to be as bad as they thought it was, it is a real luxury to them. It does them good to their very bones. Nothing gives them half so much pleasure. They slide down the sides of it as men slide down the sides of frozen mountains. To roll over and over upon the dung-hill of vice is their chief delight.

NATURE'S LIBRARY.

NATURE is the man's library who knows how to seek for knowledge. Nature is every man's picture gallery who knows how to hunger after and appreciate beauty.

TEMPTATION HAS A SHORT ARROW.

TEMPTATION shoots with a strong bow, but with a short arrow. If you fly high the archer cannot reach you.

DOING GOOD AT SELF-EXPENSE.

THERE is no person in this world who so uniformly takes his pay as he goes along, as he who does good at the expense of his own comfort and convenience.

INTEMPERANCE.

WE drink, not to gratify the palate, but for a business purpose. That being the case, we may begin with the milder beverages, just as we begin our fires with pine shavings, not only because we can light them so easily, but also because we want them to set on fire something solider. And wine is stepstone to brandy. Beer is stepstone the other way. It does not lead up to brandy, but it leads down to drunk, and beastly drunk.

WRINKLES.

I DO not like to see wrinkles. I think they are the devil's furrows on the brow, unless age has placed them there.

BORROWING TROUBLE.

I NEVER saw a man that could not get through a single day. If you can bear your burden to-day, if you can endure your pain to-day, you will get along well enough. You steal if you touch to-morrow. How many times have clouds rolled up in men's heaven which have apparently been full of trouble, but which have not had a trouble in them!

GOD'S CHARACTER.

IF you worship God as a being other than a God of love, you are worshiping a demon. Many a man will have to throw away his God before he can enter heaven.

WEARINESS.

DO not be weary. Do not despond. Despair is the devil to you. Hope is God's voice to you. Hope on, hold on, love on, live on.

HEAVEN, A TUNING-FORK

HEAVEN answers with us the same purpose that the tuning-fork does with the musician. Our affections are apt to get below the concert-pitch, and we take heaven to tune our hearts by.

CHILDHOOD, AN EGG.

MEN do not come into life, full-born. Childhood is but an egg laid, to be hatched by human life. Man comes into the world unfledged, and he has to work his way up through the exterior shell of ignorance, before he can peep or fly.

THE CHURCH NO MONOPOLY OF GOODNESS.

ANYTHING that is found in the church or out of the church to promote the welfare of men, has the signet of God stamping it as right, and making it divine.

CHRIST, A ROYAL ENGINEER.

NEVER lived a man to more purpose in the life that now is than Paul did. Christ was to him a royal engineer who eighteen hundred years ago cast up a highway of salvation from earth to heaven.

THE WORLD NOT A PALACE.

WHEN God built this world, He did not build a palace complete with appointments. This is a drill world. Men were not dropped down upon it like manna, fit to be gathered and used as it fell; but like seeds, to whom the plow is father, the furrow mother, and on which iron and stone, sickle, flail, and mill must act before they come to the loaf.

COMMERCIAL HONOR.

WE want to come to a higher sense of the obligation which rests upon men to keep their word and honor intact and pure to the very end.

TRUE HUMILITY.

IT is humility to think, not that you are less than somebody else, but that you are less than you ought to be.

PICTURES ON THE WINDOW.

BEHOLD in these morning pictures, wrought without color and kissed upon the window by the cold lips of Winter, another instance of that Divine Beneficence of beauty which suffuses the heavens, clothes the earth, and royally decorates the months to fill the world with joy, pure as the Great Heart from which it had its birth.

ON ONE SIDE OR THE OTHER.

EVERY man is for truth, or he is for error. Every man is for right or he is for wrong. Every man is for benevolence, or he is for selfishness. Every man is for the spiritual, or he is for the animal.

VALUE OF THE CHURCH.

WITH all its faults, is there anything that aims so high as the Church; is there any other thing that could fill the void if it should sink?

CHRISTIAN MANHOOD.

WHEN a man means religion there is no need that he should miss religion. A man that means manhood has a road broad enough for a fool to find out at midnight.

RESIGNATION.

LET no one sound the keynote of his own desire first, and ask nature to take up the harmony. Let him accept clouds when clouds are sent, sunlight when sunlight comes; little things— rude things—all things.

GOD'S KINGDOM NOT A PLACE.

JESUS taught that the kingdom of God is not a place, but a moral condition, and that anybody who reaches up to that moral condition is a member of that kingdom.

EMPTY SHIPS.

SOME men are like empty ships, which dance and toss about like egg-shells on the water, but which, if you load them, and sink them down to the deck, will ride steadily through the waves. Many men have to experience real trouble before they will carry an even keel; and then they make good voyages. In the case of not a few, real trouble is the best thing that can happen to them. Many men are like old pastures which are very short and turf-bound, which do not like to be plowed, but the usefulness of which, as is shown by the crops they produce, is materially increased by their being turned over to the depth of fifteen inches or so. Many men do not like to have their old soddy lives plowed up by trouble, but their lives are improved, as is shown by the clarifying effects porduced upon them, by being turned up from the very bottom.

SUPPLE DOGS.

TO be pressed down by adversity is not a disgrace; but it *is* a disgrace to lie down under it like a supple dog.

TRUST IN GOD.

MANY persons trust God just as many cities light their streets, which, when the moon shines brightly, are very particular to light all their gas-lights; but which, when the moon is gone, neglect to light them at all. I have seen men who, when in prosperity, were strong in their trust in God, but who, when surrounded by adverse circumstances, had no trust in God or anything else.

HONEST THIEVES.

OH, thou honest legal thief! God writes thee down a fitter tenant of the jail than yonder culprit! The unwhipped crimes of men undetected, are often worse than the crimes that officers make known and punish.

UNDERSTANDING POWER.

THE quality and the quantity of the understanding power in man, determines how much can be revealed to him.

THE MISERY OF WEALTH.

MEN that have wealth and do not know what to do with it, are the most miserable men out of hell—and they ought to be! There is a fable told of a man whose gold was poured molten down his throat. The same thing is done every day in the year among us; and we hear the victims squeal perpetually in their wretchedness and misery.

PAUL AND MOSES.

I SUPPOSE there never was a man equal to Paul—not even Moses. When I discourse about Moses I am sure that he is the greatest man that ever lived; and when I discourse about Paul, I know that he is the greatest man that ever lived. Let these two men stand side by side. They are fit brothers, the one as a representative of the old dispensation, the other as a representative of the new dispensation; the one a leader in the reign of muscle; the other a leader in the reign of the spirit. These two men stand head and shoulders above any other men that ever lived since the time of Christ. Indeed, they are more than all the other men that have lived since that time, throwing in even the prophets.

A DOUBTFUL BENEFIT.

AN education that threads down the constitution of a child is a very doubtful benefit.

OCCASIONAL MEDITATION.

NOW the power of this world to teach us of God, and to bring us into communion with Him, is not to be rendered available to us by an occasional meditation upon it, nor by reading a chapter of *Hervey's Meditations,* or anybody else's meditations; nor by looking, now and then, out of our windows, on Sundays, at the world.

DOWNY LIES.

THERE are different sizes of feathers on an eagle; there are wing-feathers, and tail-feathers and down. And there are wing-feather lies, and downy lies. You can lie without opening your mouth, as well as by opening it. Your little finger can lie as well as your tongue.

REASONING UP.

ALWAYS reason up, never down. Under any circumstances, never allow yourselves to say, "But may I not do this?" Never say to yourself: "Has not this been tied too tight?" I say a man who is just as good as the law makes him, is a mean man.

TEXTS FROM LIFE.

WHEN our Saviour preached, He never took a text out of the Bible, except in one instance—namely, when He preached His opening sermon in the synagogue. On all other occasions He took His texts out of life. And what a commentary is this fact upon those who say that we must not bring anything into the pulpit out of ordinary daily life, or anything which is not taken out of the Bible—a notion which is anti-Christian, and against the example of Christ, *as well as against common sense!*

JUNE.

JUNE! Rest! This is the year's bower. Sit down within it. Wipe from thy brow the toil. The elements are thy servant. The earth shows thee all her treasure.

The wonder is that every other man is not, in the month of June, a gentle fanatic. Floral insanity is one of the most charming inflictions to which man is heir..

CHRYSALIS MEN.

NO man has a right to say, "I will take the regality of power which I have, and carve out a place, and store it with abundance, and go in there and enjoy myself for the rest of my life." The life of such a man is the insect life. There is a worm to begin with. This worm goes into himself to take his ease, and becomes a dead, juicy chrysalis. A worm, a butterfly, a sack of juice: these are the three forms of insect life. And how many men are there that are worms in their beginnings, who, when they have gone through their crawling period, wing their way in the summer warmth for a time, and then go back into a substantial chrysalis state!

MARRYING GODS.

ALL women marry gods, but sadly consent afterwards to live with men.

TENDER AS A WOMAN.

HE was as tender as a woman—or rather, I should have said, he lacked the toughness of a woman; for, slender and shrinking as women are, when troubles come they are almost the only persons who are tough of heart. They are tender of skin, but inside they are as strong as iron.

DISORDERED STOMACHS.

THERE are a great many temptations that are mere nervous temptations, and a great many visions that are simply improper manifestations of the mental economy. There are a great many things which men register in their journals as the work of the Devil, that are nothing but the work of a disordered stomach.

LYMAN BEECHER.

HIS example was one which inspired faith in manhood, in disinterested affection and unfeigned piety. He seemed a good and true man, but he was better than he seemed.

CAUSE AND EFFECT.

TO deny the evidence of cause and effect in geology is to deny the only principle on which you can demonstrate the existence of a God.

RELIGION LIKE A BIRD.

DO you suppose that religion is like a bird in a cage, and that you can lock it up in the church, and that the keeper will take care of it, and feed it, and have it ready to sing for you whenever you chose to come here and listen to it? Is that your idea of religion? Very well, then; your Bible and mine are different. We read different translations!

A PROVERB.

IT has passed into a proverb that before election, "condescension to men of low estate," is the very fullness of the Bible. They esteem every man a brother, and would esteem every woman a sister if she only had a vote.

PEDIGREE FARMERS.

THEN there are the pedigree farmers, not unknown among men in natural husbandry. They have got the very poorest fruit to be found in the whole neighborhood, bearing the highest sounding names. They have got the most marvelous pears, the most wonderful apples, the most extraordinary strawberries. They give the most astonishing names to the most meagre, miserable fruit. But then, it has such high-sounding titles! There are these same men whose herds are about the poorest, the scrawniest, and the weakest in the whole country round about them; but they have a pedigree that takes them back, every one of them, to Noah's Ark! Their oxen are lean, their cows are milkless, but they are proud of them nevertheless, they have such a noble pedigree! They are uncurried, unfatted, and unfatable, to be sure; but ah, what a line of blood did they spring from! Did you never see just such husbandmen in the Church? —men who had no greater morality, or piety, or spiritual experience, but who went back through a long pedigree, one going plump up to Peter, and another plump up to Paul, and others plump up to the prophets themselves!

A LIBRARY.

A LITTLE library growing larger every year is an honorable part of a young man's history. It is a man's duty to have books. A library is not a luxury, but one of the necessaries of life.

SLEEPING IN CHURCH.

IN what other painful event of life has a good man so little sympathy as when overcome with sleep in meeting time? In his lawful bed a man cannot sleep, and in his pew he cannot keep awake!

AUTUMNAL COLORS

OUR English friends have seen autumnal colors, but when they have once seen a color-autumn in America, how imperfect do they find their conceptions to have been!

OVERWORK.

HOW many do we now see among us who are dragging themselves along through life, reaping the inevitable consequences of an overtaxed body, because they esteem business and profits above health and comfort. They say, "I would fain stop, but I can see no place to stop." By-and-by, when disease takes you by the shoulders and pitches you on the bed, I think you will find a place to stop! When the undertaker comes along you will find a place to stop!

OCTOBER.

OCTOBER! Orchard of the year! Ripened seeds shake in their pods. Apples drop in the stillest hours. The days are calm. The nights are tranquil.

It is a little saddening though to have a month in which the whole garden might have gone on growing, with all its tassels and fringes, its cups and clusters, but for that single solitary night.

CONTENTMENT.

IF a man has come to that point where he is content, he ought to be put in his coffin; for a contented live man is a sham!

CHILDISHNESS.

IT would be better for us if we had more childishness about ourselves. Masons know that that work is never good which sets too quick. If manhood sets too quick, it is apt to be stiff and brittle.

LANDSCAPE GARDENING.

THE true landscape gardener is an artist who should rank with the masters. He uses trees for forms and colors, not on a canvas, but on the wide fields.

MARTIN LUTHER.

MARTIN LUTHER asks no leave of pope or emperor now. He is the monarch of thought, and the noblest defender of the faith to the end of time.

REMNANTS.

YOU know that in the business of publishing there are what are called "the remainders." If an edition of a book is published, and it is not all sold, the part that remains unsold is called "the remainder" of that edition. And in manufacturing establishments and stores there is a great amount of stock which is called "remnants," and which consists of scraps, and shop-worn goods that are left over. Now I think that the church and the community are full of "remnants" and "remainders"—men that are left over.

ASKING AMISS.

GOD, who loves us so well, will no more permit us to mark out the things which we are to have, than a parent will say to a child, "What do you want?" and then promise to give it what it asks for. It would want the razors, the tempting bottles of medicine, the wine and brandy, (till it had tasted them!) and such like things.

LEFT OUT OF DOORS.

THIS world was made for poor men, and therefore, the greater part of it was left out of doors, where everybody could enjoy it.

INTELLIGENCE.

IF a man has nothing better to do than turning a grindstone, it is better to be educated; or sticking pins on a paper, or sweeping the streets; it makes no difference what you do, you will do it better if you are an intelligent man. It is said that blood will tell in stock; and I know that intelligence will tell in man.

STAVING OFF JUDGMENT.

I TELL you that the moral reasonings of the store and the counting-room, with reference to what is right and what is wrong in getting money, and the reasonings of God's judgment-seat, will be very different operations. You can muzzle your fear, and you can silence your conscience, and you can go on making money by ways which God abhors, and which every honest man ought to abhor, and you can, in the meantime, have comparative peace; but there is a great difference between staving off judgment now, and staving off revelation and judgment then!

BOTH WORTHLESS.

THE supine sluggard is no more indolent than the bustling do-nothing.

FORTUNE SEEKING.

THE stories tell us about men who go out to *seek* their fortunes, but in America the term *work out* is better.

PROGRESS OF THE RACE.

MANKIND are yet to be enfranchised. God's power will break through and shatter all combinations that undertake to hinder the onward progress of the race.

LUCK.

THE fool's luck, lottery luck, good-fortune luck, superstitious luck—do not trust to that. Luck is in the heart, the head, and the hand.

THE WORLD A GRINDSTONE.

THE world is a grindstone, and races are axes which are to get their cutting edges by being ground on it! The very object for which God thinks it worth while to turn and roll this round globe, is that by its very attrition and working, men may be made men in every sense of the term.

SAVING POWER OF LOVE.

WHETHER a man be high church, or low church, or new church, or no church; whether he hold this creed, or that creed, or no creed, if he has the saving power of love in the soul, grace be upon him.

ON PREACHING.

NOW there are thousands that derive intellectual pleasure from preaching. T' are-like to hear the sound of the music, which shows that the parade is coming. By and by, in comes the preacher, and he develops his soldiers' ideas to their great admiration, and parades them through a long sermon. When he is done, the people, as they go out, say, "Splendid parade, wasn't it? Fine ideas—fine ideas? Very well put." To whom were they put? There wasn't a musket that had a ball or any powder in it. Not a man dreamed of hitting anybody. It was a sham; all a sham. There was no fight. The sermon was all a mere exhibition of ideas, a mere marching of ideas.

THE GATE OPEN.

WHEN you come to the gate of heaven, you may be sure, if you knock, and say, "Lord, Lord, open unto me," that you will not get in. A man that is fit to go in, always goes up without dreaming that God will not let him in. He expects to find the gate open.

LOVE.

LOVE never cares for what it gets, but oh, how it rejoices in what it gives!

HOW MERCIES ARE TREATED.

MOST men treat their mercies as I have seen persons treat flowers that I had given them. They took them with an indifferent "Thank you," but seemed to regard them as so many mere leaves, or as some miserable, worthless things, and presently commenced picking them to pieces; and by the time they had taken twenty steps the walk was strewn with fragments of them, and I looked after them and said, "If you get another gift from me, you will know it."

THE TRINITY.

YOU may quarrel about the Trinity. I let the Trinity take care of itself. You say it is taught in the Bible. All right. But as I know nothing about it, I simply accept the fact and go on.

NOT YET BORN.

THE experiences of love are such sometimes, even in this life, as to be an earnest, a blessed interpretation, of something more glorious yet to come. There is one thing which the New Testament is always in labor with, and which is never born, and that is the conception of the greatness of the love of Christ to our souls.

LOVE OF FLOWERS.

IF you do not love your garden enough to care for it as you would for a baby, better let it alone. Flowers will not be put off with arm's length cordiality.

CROAKERS.

AND that whole owl set of men, that raven, black-winged-prophet set, that sit on the dry branches of nature, and croak about this miserable world and this miserable life, belong outside of the line of Christianity. Not only are they not disciples of Christ, but they are not knowledgeable men even in the elements of Christianity.

HEAD DAYS—HEART DAYS.

SOME days seem to be characterized by some single sense. There are head-days, heart-days, there are eye-days and ear-days, and promiscuous days in which delicious sensations of pleasure at life in general predominate.

SUNDAY WITH MY AUNT.

ONE Sunday afternoon with my Aunt Esther did me more good than forty Sundays in church with my father. He thundered over my head, and she sweetly instructed me down in my heart.

GOOD, SOLID DOCTRINES.

NOW let a minister, for nineteen sermons out of twenty, preach of abstract doctrines, that neither he nor God knows anything about, because they are not true, and the people would say, "Here is a man who knows how to lay down good, solid doctrines. He is a great preacher."

OBEDIENCE IN CHILDREN.

IT is a cruel kindness to leave a child's disposition unsubdued. One who has never learned how to obey, will be at fault all his life long. It is a vital attainment. Flax is no better than any weed, unless it be broken, hatcheled; then it may be spun and woven; then it may be manufactured and worn.

YOU HAVE ME THERE.

WE do not know precisely what our being will be in the future, though we know in general. I know in general what the Aurora Borealis is. If you press the question as to what it is, I say, "It is a bank of tremulous, up-mounting light, at the North." If you ask, "What is it made of?" you have me there.

GOD'S LAWS ETERNAL.

THE constable sleeps, and the sheriff nods, and the judge is unknowing; but the laws of God follow a man by night and by day, and never leave him.

GOOD NATURE.

GOOD nature is not to be an occasional thing, which a man summons once in a while, as he does his doctor or his attorney.

HIDDEN THOUGHTS.

"THE thoughts which are hidden are the most precious The shells which the sea rolls out on shore are not its best. The pearls have to be dived for."

PROFITABLE MISTAKES

OUR successes are not so profitable to us as our mistakes. It is a comfort to believe that our mistakes in this world will have rectification in the world to come—as they will.

WRONG DOING FOR OTHERS.

BE careful of doing wrong to your employers, and be just as firm never to do any wrong for them as you are never to do any wrong against them. No matter if they wish a whiplash, and wish to strike it out, never let them tie you to the handle.

DICKENS.

DICKENS' books, though they are not theological or religious, are books which are in strange and admirable harmony with this message, "GOOD WILL TO MEN."

THE NEW YEAR.

EVERY man should be born again on the first of January. Take up one hole more in the buckle or let down one, but on the first of the year let every man gird himself anew with his face to the front.

LIFE'S TRAGEDIES.

I THINK, indeed, the great tragedies of life are not to be found by going to the theatre, but often by staying at home. There is not a week in which there are not tragedies enacted that are more effecting than any that literature has ever embalmed. There is hardly a family in which, watched from year to year, there are not things, rightly taken, rightly judged and appreciated, more exquisite than anything represented by art, or by tragedy—things that are simply indescribable. I see them; and while, as yet, the impression is fresh upon me, I say to myself, "Ah, if I might but preach now, how I could set the truth forth!" But it fades.

When the farmer rises in the morning, and sees upon the windows the most exquisite art, the etching of frost-pictures he wonders how nature, in her careless mood, can work out that which it would be the ambition of the deftest hand in the world to do; and as he looks, it dissolves before his breath. The warmth of his presence destroys it all. I look upon human experiences, from place to place, transiently, evanescently, and, as it were, the very warmth of my feeling effaces them. I cannot describe them. Who does not know a great many such cases? Look at the bounties of some, the charity and lenity of others, the justice against one's self of others, the self-denial and burden-bearing, here and there, of yet others. Why, life is full of these things. Because they are not put upon a pedestal, and because men are not shouting their praises, we are apt to suppose that acts of heroism are occasional.

INACTIVITY.

A MAN rusts out more by inactivity in a year than he wears out by wholesome activity in a lifetime. A man's sum of enjoyment depends upon what he has in himself.

BENEFIT OF IDEALS.

IDEALS make blessed discontent; not murmuring, not repining, but aspiration. A love for that which is better is divine in man.

LIMBER-BACKED.

IF we have once come to the habit of feeling vigorous and intense disapprobation of things evil, we shall be in but little danger of being drawn astray by them. But no man can come into such a habit, who is limber-backed in his disposition.

CONTENTMENT.

ACCEPT your lot as a man does a piece of rugged ground, and begin to get out the rocks and roots to deepen and mellow the soil, to enrich and plant it.

NATURE'S HINTS OF GRACE.

WHERE is a very limited hint in nature of the provisions of grace. There is a very limited idea of atonement and of regeneration in nature. A broken bone will grow together again. There is in nature, in certain stages, and up to certain points, a kind of provision for restoration from mischiefs; but beyond that there is no provision at all. Let a man take a teaspoonful of prussic acid, and then let him get back to his former state if he can.

SANCTIFIED PEOPLE.

IF God were to blow the trumpet to-day and call only sanctified persons, there would not be one to march under His banner.

IMMORTALITY.

WE are all marching thither. We are all going home. Men shiver at the idea that they are going to die; but this world is only a nest. We are scarcely hatched out of it here. We do not know ourselves. We have strange feelings that do not interpret themselves. The mortal in us is crying out for the immortal. As in the night, the child, waking with some vague and nameless terror, cries out to express its fear and dread, and its cry is interpreted in the mother's heart, who runs to the child and lays her hand upon it, and quiets it to sleep again. So do you not suppose that the ear of God hears our disturbances and trials and tribulations in life? Do you not suppose that He who is goodness itself cares for you? Do you suppose that He whose royal name is Love has less sympathy for you than a mother has for her babe? Let the world rock. If the foot of God is on the cradle, fear not. Look up, take courage, hope, and hope to the end.

THOUGHTS—FEELINGS—DESIRES.

A MAN is what he thinks, a man is what he feels, a man is what he desires.

NATURE GOD'S PHENOMENA.

IS Nature mere phenomena? Or is it God's phenomena, meant to convey something deeper than the body catches—something for the soul?

GIVING ADVICE.

MEN are always willing to give advice. Sometimes it is wise to take it from one's neighbors.

OBSCURE HEROES.

THERE is great deal of heroism in the shop, and in the very streets of life; for whoever does right in spite of temptation; whoever endures patiently in spite of the annoyances of life; whoever, knowing that neither the trumpet nor the newspaper will ever know anything about it, as in the sight of God and only in the sight of God, not appreciated nor even known among men, maintains, for Christ's sake, the beauty of moral quality, is a hero, although he is an obscure one. Oh, the unregarded heroes! Oh, the mothers that sacrifice themselves for their children! Oh, the children that deny themselves every inducement to exaltation and to future prosperity, to care for their aged parents, giving up every one of the ambitions of life! All those that in lowly places are seeking to follow after Christ, are heroes; and their heroism will one day flash out and be revealed.

VALUE OF SUFFERING.

THERE is triumph where there is suffering that has self-denial in it, and where that self-denial means the emancipation of nobler elements from the bondage of lower ones.

A WISE MAXIM.

GEN. GRANT'S words, "When is the time to show a man's self friendly except when his friend has made a mistake?" Form one of those moral principles that address themselves to the universal conscience.

BORN INTO SPEAKING.

I REMEMBER very well, when I was born into speaking. I had made faint efforts at writing; but there were wise men that edited the Boston *Recorder* then, and they did not print what I wrote. I remember feeling desperate about it. But I remember, in a little debating society—The Hamiltonian,—standing up to say a few things I had prepared to say; and the impulse came on me, such as I never felt before, but shall never cease to feel as long as I live; and I astonished myself, and astonished all the boys around me, too. They did not dream that any such stream could come out of such a well as that! And from that day to this that impulse never died—the being born into the knowledge and consciousness and certainty that I had it in me to speak. It never stopped.

A LOCK OF HAIR.

WE are children that know very little about our Father. I am not superstitious, but I believe in talismans. I have a lock of auburn hair—my mother's. It connects me with her. Doubtless my little hands lay upon her head. She nursed me upon her bosom. All my life she has been my stay. To me that lock of hair is worth more than gold or jewels. To my outward and physical man, perhaps, it is not worth anything, but to my inward man, my sentimental nature, it is without price. All precious things could not equal it. I never saw her except as a babe; I was a three-year-old child when she died; and therefore I have no association personally with her. Some few filmy and flitting things remain in my babyhood's memory ; but this connects me with her. It is a cord stronger than silver or gold, iron or steel could be made.

Now, I am also a child of God; and when I gather together all the best ideas of Him they are not much more than enough to make a lock of His hair; but they hold me to Him. There is to come a disclosure of Him that is so transcendent that now there is not only no language for it, but no foundation in human consciousness for it. Our conceit leads us all the time to think that we can picture the secret of truth, and measure its circumference and diameter. We can take the measurement of limited things; but that egotism which leads us to suppose we can measure God, so that we can fully comprehend Him, is our supreme mistake.

AGES LIKE FAMILY GROUPS.

AGES are like family groups : they had better mind their own business, and not mind that of others; therefore it is an impertinence for one age to discuss those great principles which belong to another.

LIKE A SHIP.

MANY think that the church is like a ship, that never should leak or change its form on the voyage. If anything happens on board, everybody expects fire, or flood, or some great disaster.

FIRST EFFORTS AT GOODNESS.

MOST men's first efforts at goodness are very crooked and shallow, like a man's furrow in a newly plowed piece of ground: hit or miss, and oftener miss.

TWO VIEWS OF GOD.

THE two views are these: one says that God built the world as a house, and that He is master of the house; and the other says He built the world as a house, and then locked himself out.

HEADLIFE—HEARTLIFE.

THE life of some men is so much in the heart that if you were to cut off their heads they would'nt miss much; and the life of others is so much in the head that you could almost take out their heart and they wouldn't miss much.

FATHERHOOD.

WHAT would you think of an earthly father who was so perfect that his children could not possibly have anything in common with him; who was so perfect that he was above their infantile sports; who was too wise to talk of their infantile follies; who felt too deeply to have sympathy with their little feelings; and who had no connection with their incipient life, and rude, imperfect ways? Would such a character be admirable in a father? He might as well be carved out of marble; or he might as well be Maelzel's automaton, and with turned crank, or wound-up spring, work out all the duties he owes to his family!

FAME.

THERE are some things by which a man can connect himself with his time. In material things there may be artists and engineers that are conscious of their inspiration, and that work not without a dim consciousness that their names will be known. I do not believe that Michael Angelo, or Raphael, or Giorgione, or Titian, or Correggio, was without those thoughts. So one may build a bridge, as a man of illustrious name built the Brooklyn Bridge, and may be conscious, as well he may be, "This will carry my name down to immortality." A man who sings a song, or gives musical wings to a hymn, that it may fly over all the earth, carrying courage and joy, love and peace, may, as Watts, Doddridge, and Charles Wesley might have done, say, "I never shall be forgotton so long as breath remains to mankind." So long as any tear is to be wiped away by the lyrics of the soul, such men will not be forgotten. They felt it, and so they sang; and not from ambition, but from the irresistible impulse of song, they will be immortal.

THE DEVIL LONG-HEADED.

I THINK no man ever cheated the devil, and I think no man ever will. I have no doubt that the devil overreaches himself and cheats himself; but in any transaction between you and him, he is longer-headed than you are.

THE KEY OF NATURE.

IT is as right for some persons to have the chamber of the soul unlocked by the key of nature, as for them to have it unlocked by the key of the catechism.

JOHN BROWN.

JOHN BROWN felt that his whole life was good for nothing except as an offering to others. He went to death as men go to a banquet, and as he was led forth to the sacrifice he kissed a little child.

LOVE LIKE RINGING BELLS.

I THINK it is one of the hardest things in the world to say, I love you. I don't know why. A man who could look a woman in the face and say, I love you, without shrinking, ought to shrink. Love is like the ringing of bells; they sound sweetly while they are chiming; but after all it is hard work to ring them. And I marvel at the deep, manly and tender love which Christ poured out upon His disciples. They found in Him united both father and mother.

GREEDY MEN.

THERE are many men so greedy that they feel what their neighbors make, that they might have made, is taken away from them; and that they have lost all that they do not get of what they meant to get. Their eyes grow large, their imagination becomes fevered, and they mean to rush over the course and scoop up wealth by the armful; but they lose their judgment and accuracy before they know it, and stumble, and measure their whole length in the dust, on the ground.

THOUGHTS ABOUT SELF.

IT is a bad thing for a man to think too much about himself, to talk too much about himself, or to examine himself too much. The less he indulges in these things the better he is off. Let a man have a sense of duty, and take a right direction in life, and then sweep and lunge toward things outward as much as possible.

THE RIGHT OF SPEECH

"I HAVE a right to think, to speak, and to do." But you have the other right, also, to hold your tongue. You are not bound to speak whenever you have a mind to.

PRAYER.

A PRAYER is not a thread upon which men are to see how many texts they can string.

CRITICISM AND SATIRE.

TO watch to see what is awkward in others; to search out the infirmities of men; to go out like a street-sweeper, or a universal scavenger, to collect the faults and failings of people; to carry these things about as if they were cherries or flowers; to throw them out of your bag or pouch, and make them an evening repast or a noonday meal, or the amusement of a social hour, enlivened by unfeeling criticisms, heartless jests, and cutting sarcasms; to take a man up as you would a chicken, and gnaw his flesh from his very bones, and then lay him down, saying, with fiendish exultation, "There is his skeleton" —this is devilish!

THE TEST OF MANHOOD.

WHO cannot do things that are so easy that they do themselves? The test of manhood is the power to do with cheerfulness things that are difficult and disagreeable.

BUTS AND IFS.

NEVER, when you see a thing to be right, stand shaking and quaking, and say, "But then." That "but then" is a devil damned. *If* and *but* have destroyed more souls than any fiend in hell.

THE ROMAN CATHOLIC CHURCH.

I LOOK upon the Roman Catholic Church as being dead in one branch and another, and as being bark-bound and worm-eaten, but as having some real good sap in it yet, and some living boughs, and as bearing some fair fruit; and I can say, "God be thanked for the good in the Roman Catholic Church." "But," says one, "do you think one religious system as good as another?" By no manner of means. There are systems that seem to me to be wonderfully adapted to avoid the evil and promote the good, and to be as much better than some other systems as a mason's trowel is better than a chip with which to lay brick in a wall.

LIFE, A HULL OF SELFISHNESS.

MEN have a little boat of piety, which runs up and down the waves of their experience; but their life is a great hull of selfishness, the bow of which is rigged with the lower passions.

DREAMING OF RICHES.

THOUSANDS of boys are dreaming of growing suddenly rich—and I call a man a boy as long as he is foolish; so that the boyhood of a great many, you see, goes with them clear through life! There are thousands of boys, of all ages, that are dreaming about going to bed poor, and waking up rich.

FALLING FROM GRACE.

"IF a man falls and it don't hurt him much, it wan't grace he fell from. A feller's apt to be smashed up if he falls from grace, I tell ye."

THE AIR OF THE FUTURE WORLD.

IT is how much of the invisible we can bring into this life that makes this life rich and valuable. I will tell you a secret of gardening. Turnips and other crops that have long roots, and depend mostly for their nourishment on the soil, exhaust the soil; while those crops that have broad leaves, and take the greater portion of their nourishment from the air, organizing it, and turning it into the soil, enrich the soil. Now let me tell you that that which makes this life rich is that broad-leaved experience which derives its support from the air of the future world.

MEN LIKE TULIPS

I THINK God makes men, in some respects, as he makes tulips. In the autumn of the year the next year's blossom is stored up, all ready to come forth, and there is food enough in it to get it out of the ground. Children are bulbs. There is parent enough in them to last till they can organize character for themselves.

THE TONGUE.

OH, commend me to that man who carries his dagger in his hand, and not in his mouth! Commend me to that man who only dips his dagger in poison which the apothecary can make, and who does not dip it in the infernal, rancorous poison which Satan brews! There are men that we have seen, the flap of whose tongue, not in a single instance merely, but in scores of instances, makes the difference between heaven on earth and hell on earth.

PERSONAL SLANDEROUS REPORTS.

IT matters not if men roll my name about in slanderous reports, as a boy would roll a foot-ball down a dirty street, so long as the cause of God succeeds.

WHAT IS NOT PROMISED.

GOD does not promise that if a man shuts himself off from the world, and prays, and sings, and reads good books, and neglects his worldly business, that he will make up to him all that he loses by such neglect. When a man opens a store on Broadway, God does not say to him, "Now, you have rented your building, and purchased your goods, and hired your clerks; and if you will go back into your counting-room, and spend your time in reading, and singing, and praying, I will see to the fore part of the store."

GOD'S PROVIDENCE.

THERE is a providence of God, a thinking of God for us; but it is no such providence or thinking as ever takes the place of, or interferes with, our own personal wisdom. There is a providence of God, but it never weaves cloth.

A LETTER OF CREDIT.

NOW God gives to every man a circular letter of credit for life, and says; "Whenever you get to a place where you need assistance, take your letter to the Banker and the needed assistance will be given you."

LIFE A FLIGHT OF STAIRS.

WE are living on a flight of stairs in this world, and we shall not touch the chamber floor till we touch the vestibule of heaven.

THE BIBLE A PLAIN BOOK.

WHAT a coarse book this Bible is. It has never been to school to get refined, so we have to take it just as we find it. These are plain words: "If a man say, I love God, and hateth his brother, he is a liar. For he that loveth not his brother, whom he hath seen, how can he love God, whom he hath not seen?" Show me a man that is proud and over-reaching, who professes to be pious, and I will tell you that his piety is all flummery. There is not a bit of piety in such a man.

DEEDS OF KINDNESS.

DEEDS of kindness must not be occasional, and as enforced duties; they must be the spontaneous acts of an abiding disposition of Christian love. They must grow out of you as grass grows out of the summer-warmed ground. You don't have to coax grass to grow; you can't coax it not to grow.

A DEVIL INSIDE.

IF Satan be clothed like an angel of light, and every feather in his wing be of silver or of gold, he is the devil inside, notwithstanding.

BETRAYING CHRISTIANS.

IT is not in the power of all the Bolingbrokes, and Voltaires, and Tom Paines, and Rousseaus, and other great names that write infidel matters—it is not in the power of all the locust hosts of infidels—to do that damage to true religion which may be done by an unfaithful church, or by the ungodly testimony, in practical life, of professors of religion; for betraying Christians are the devil's colporteurs, who peddle tracts of infidelity; not printed tracts, but living epistles—their own examples.

GENIUS AND INDUSTRY.

GENIUS needs industry as much as industry needs genius.

THE OIL OF GRACE.

NOW, if a man brings his thoughts and feelings into higher Christian experience, when he takes them out, his piety is all radiant; but no sooner is it brought in contact with the world than its radiancy is lost. Therefore there is no figure in the Bible that I am aware of which compares the Christian to a coal of fire, or glowing iron. He is always compared to a torch, or to a lamp that will never burn low if you keep it supplied with oil. We are, as Christians, to keep ourselves supplied with the oil of grace.

REVIVAL CONVERTS.

NOW, there are many who enlist on the parade-ground of revivals, with the expectation that when they come out they will be happy, and feel good all their life.

STRIKING BOTTOM.

THERE is many a man who, when he struck bottom, thanked God for it—though he cried all the way down.

MODERATION.

THERE is a kind of moderation that is in the mind what perfect health is in the organs of the body. And there is a kind of greediness that overlays success. If a bird should seek to hasten forward its young by putting its eggs in an oven, they might be roasted, but they would not be hatched any sooner.

BEACONS.

THERE are some men who seem to be continued in life to serve as beacons of warning, rather than guiding lights, to those around them. It would be difficult to tell what a great many men who are in communities live for, or what they do; and among these you will generally find those who say, "The world owes us a living." The world owes them a living for what? For being paupers in it; for being drudges; for being moths that consume, instead of productive insects that multiply, as bees do, the stock.

NO BETTER THAN A BUG.

IF I am only that which I have been, I am of all men most miserable. I am no better than a leaf, no better than the bug that is on it.

STARTING RIGHT.

AFTER a man has once commenced life, he cannot go back and start again. He cannot rid himself of his responsibilities, and take an entirely new set of papers, and begin anew.

MAN NOT AN OYSTER.

WHEN God wanted sponges and oysters, he made them, and put one on a rock, and the other in the mud. When he made man, he did not make him to be a sponge or an oyster; he made him with feet, and hands, and head, and heart, and vital blood, and a place to use them, and said to him, "Go! work!"

NO NEED OF A DEVIL.

THE strongest evidence I can think of against there being a devil, is that there is no need of one. Men do works of evil in such abundance that there would seem to be nothing left for a devil to do. These things have been permitted from the beginning of the world to our day, and by a Being who is said to be too good to let an evil spirit live! But when I look at the facts, this namby-pamby talk about the impossibility of God's creating a principle of evil is simply contemptible to me. A man who has not nerve, and brawn and bone enough to look at things as they are, and admit them, I don't know what business such a man has to live!

NOVELS AS PREACHERS.

EVEN novels are becoming preachers; and better preachers than are many pulpits. For the novels of the last fifteen or twenty years contain a better Gospel than the pulpits, if you include the pulpits of the Greek Church, of the Roman Church, of formal Protestantism, and of the warring sects. A dead Gospel is a hideous heresy.

LIKE A MAY MORNING.

THERE are men who smell like a May morning all through the business hours of the day. They save their ugliness for their wife and children at home.

CARE A NETTLE-HEDGE.

TO be in perfect health, one must be in such a condition that he does not know that there is anything of him. Now suppose a man is sound in every organ, but that in the morning he goes through a nettle-hedge, what effect does it have upon him? Why, although he is in good health, although his lungs are right, and his heart is right, and his nerves are right, and every other part of his body is right, yet, all day long he is chafed, and fretted, and irritated, just because in the morning he went through that nettle-hedge. Well, care is to the mind what nettles are to the body.

MEN LIKE HARPS.

MEN are not music-boxes, which, when wound up, carry their own players inside of them; but they are harps, which must be touched from without. Each man's heart, therefore, must be touched by other men. We are to touch other men's hearts. Other men's hearts are belfries, and there we must ring out all our chimes.

HERESY HUNTERS.

THERE are in the Church what may be called heresy-hunters. They always carry a rifle, a spiritual rifle, under their arm. You will find them forever outlying, watching for heresy, not so much in their own hearts, not so much in their own church, not so much in their own ministers, but in other people's hearts, and other people's churches, and other people's ministers. If any man happens to hold an opinion respecting any doctrine which does not accord with their own peculiar views, they are spread abroad to run him down. They are taking care of, and defending, the faith! They are searching for foxes, and wolves, and bears, that they suppose are laying waste God's husbandry! They never do anything except fire at other folks and other things. I have no doubt that Nimrod was a very good fellow, in his own poor, miserable way; but a Nimrod minister is the meanest of all sorts of hunters!

OX-LIKE BRAINS.

A MAN whose brain puts him alongside of the ox may low till the judgment day, but he will not be more than an ox.

IF I HAD ONLY KNOWN.

THEY are always saying, "If I had only known." They are like the farmer who, having lost his crop from want of diligence in the Spring, went to harrowing and hoeing in November, to regain what he had lost, but who, failing in the attempt, said, "Oh, if I had only done right in the Spring!" It is enough that you made a fool of yourself in the Spring. Because you made a fool of yourself in the Spring, is no reason why you should make a fool of yourself again in the Autumn.

DO-NOTHINGS.

PERSONS there are who go tagging after meetings all the time, and doing nothing themselves.

INFLUENCE.

YOUR influence is working for light or for darkness, for purity or impurity, for good or for evil.

IDLENESS.

WHEN Satan would put men to a crop of mischief, he finds the idle man already prepared, and has scarcely the trouble of sowing.

HOW TO TREAT DIRT.

IN the collisions of men pushed on by pleasure, or ambition, or avarice, there is a constant play and counter-play of petty provocations, petty tales, mean deceptions, ungrateful supplantings, repaying fairness with foulness, honor with dishonesty. Now a noble mind rids himself of these wrongs as he does his garments of spattered mud. He lets them alone while fresh, since brushing would only spread them. He waits till they dry, and then cleanses himself of them all, and lets the dirt fall back to the dirt.

SOUL COMMERCE.

I SEE young people going, after marriage, to set up housekeeping. They go together and select a house where they shall live, and discuss it—it is very sweet and beautiful. They go together to the upholsterer, and agree upon the carpets, the curtains, and all the other furnishings. It is a charming little time that they have together. Those are points in one's life that are very pleasing, very agreeable, and that ought not to be forgotten. They live together, furnishing the house; and then they go for books—for fashion requires that men should have some books somewhere. They go together, also, for engravings, for etchings, for paintings, and for a little jewelry. So they set up their housekeeping. Then they say, "Now then, we must invite company; we must form a circle of friends." With many little disagreements that set them slightly apart they select; and they have parties, and go to parties, and enlarge the bounds of their outside life; and then when two or three years have passed away, what have they done for housekeeping inside? Has he more generosity? and did she create it? Has she more patience? and did he draw it out for her? Is the strife between them, as to which shall yield to the other, or as to which shall control the other? Is it as to which shall set out the other's taste and shut up his own, or which shall insist that that one's taste shall rule? The beauty, the purity, the sweetness, and self-denial of love—oh, how many are united in these! How many persons come together by primal affection? The priest cannot do anything but put on the ring and give the blessing. Men and women are married by their own covenants to each other; and then they begin to enjoy their life together in their house, and in its employments; and then comes a larger commerce. But what commerce is going on in the crystal chamber of the soul? How are they living with each other? By what part of their nature are they living? Is there a steady ascent? Is there that ladder which Jacob saw? Yea, in many a family so poor that their pillow may be said to have been like Jacob's—a stone—there has been the ladder that lifted them up to the higher round of life, and angels have been seen ascending and descending. Blessed are the poor whom angels visit.

WENDELL PHILLIPS.

ALL the English-speaking people on the globe have written among the names that shall never die, the name of that scoffed, detested, mob-beaten Wendell Phillips. The men that would not defile their lips with his name are today thanking God that he lived.

CHRIST'S RESURRECTION.

JUST as the first tentative notes of waking birds began to be heard; while the leaf unshaken was yet loaded with dew; while nature was cool, and pure, and tender, as if newly made—in this early morning hour it was that Christ came forth from the sepulchre in newness of life.

FEW SEE THE ANGEL.

HOW few are there that see in their children much more than innocent little animals, at first! They see in them reasons of self-flattery further on. They see in them candidates for prosperity in life still further on Parents are proud of their children's beauty; proud of their early intelligence; proud of their grace; proud of their winsome ways in life; but how few people sit and brood upon their children as heirs of immortality! How few see the angel, or want to see it, in their children! They are the light of the household; are they the light of eternity?

DOUBLE-SIGHT.

WE must see with both eyes—the fleshly and the spiritual. Watching is the one operation; praying is the other.

NAMING CHURCHES.

I WONDER, when men are naming churches, and calling them "The Church of Divine Love," "The Church of the Holy Spirit," etc., that there has never been a church called the Church of Aspiration, the church that represents the desires of those that are longing and looking up and striving on. We have churches of the Trinity, in which we believe, but about which we know nothing; but of aspiration we know a great deal. It has not been the work of Christ to draw men up to a higher level merely in the formal acts of worship; the effect of His work has been to sweeten every element that belongs to human nature from the cradle to the coffin, from the lowest to the highest—to inspire every one of those faculties which make us men as distinguished from the animal creation. There is a climate of Jesus Christ in men; and all that is highest and best grows in that climate. Again and again we are taught that great and wonderful as has been that work of Christ whose fruits are visible, and which has filled the ages with songs and hymns and rejoicings, it is but the initial work—the beginning.

THE MEAN MAN.

I HAVE great hope of a *wicked* man; slender hope of a *mean* one.

MAN'S VIEW OF GOD.

I DO not wonder that, with the thought which most Christians have of God, they are slow to go to Him. What man would not be afraid to make prayers to a thunderbolt, if he expected that the result of every prayer would be to bring a bolt down upon his head? I should not want to charge up before the throne of God, if it were like charging before a battery.

FALSE PROPHESYING.

IF, in your prophesying, you take God's commandments, and turn them end for end, you will find yourself prophesy lies.

SOUL HEALTH.

RELIGION is to the soul what health is to the body—it is the right ordering of all the faculties. Many persons think it is confined to certain faculties, which must be set buzzing at particular times.

SMART MEN.

THERE is not one man that is smart where there are twenty men that think they are; and many men are smart only as flies are: they make a world of buzzing, but do not make much else.

MEN LIKE TREES.

MEN are like trees; each one must put forth the leaf that is created in him. Education is only like good culture—it changes the size but not the sort.

BEAUTY IN NATURE.

WHEN I am a bankrupt, and my creditor takes my house and my ground, I shall laugh at him if he thinks he has touched my properties. Above my roof are finer pictures than are under it. In the trees I have winged instruments which a sheriff will hardly catch.

EVEN BETWEEN THEM.

"THEY say he don't believe in God. Wal, I guess it's pretty even between 'em. Shouldn't wonder if God didn't believe in him neither."

WHERE MEN DWELL.

THE animal dwells where his feet are; the man where his thoughts are.

OUR DUTY TO PRACTICE.

WE not unfrequently hear men say, "It is easy for you, who have a good constitution and a happy temperament, and who are agreeably circumstanced, to do thus and so; but if you were as bilious as I am; if you were as sick as I am; if you had to contend with such trials at home as I have to; if you were a business man, and you had such a harassing business about your heels as I have about mine, you would then have as much anxiety as I have, and you would fret as much as I do. It is very easy to preach, much easier than it is to practice." I have found that out, that it is a great deal easier to preach than it is to practice; but it is nevertheless our duty to practice.

A MEMORABLE THING.

A MAN might frame and let loose a star to roll in its orbit, and yet not have done so memorable a thing before God as he who lets go a golden-orbed thought to roll through the generations of men.

MEDITATION.

MEDITATION is largely a running of the mind-mill; and it does not do any good to run the mill when there is no grist in it.

FALSE SPEAKING.

AVOID falsehood in all its varied forms, and I repeat, if you sin at all, sin on the side of truth. When men give you permission to do wrong, let it be as though they gave you permission to eat dirt. If you were told that you may eat dirt, you would say, "I don't want to eat dirt, and I won't touch it."

TRUE WISDOM.

THE wise men are those that come out best at the other end, not those that dance the nimblest at this end.

TROUBLE A SCHOOLMASTER.

THERE is one, and only one tree that bears true manhood, and that tree is trouble. Trouble is God's schoolmaster, and they who undertake to play truant will be caught. When troubles come upon you, fly higher. And if they still strike you, fly higher. And by and by they shall not be able to reach you.

RAGGED INIQUITY.

EVERYBODY sits in judgment on a dirty sin; but clean it, dress it, and polish it, and there are ten thousand people who think it is not so sinful, after all. It is ragged iniquity that is sinful; burnished iniquity is not quite so wicked.

THE WORLD AN OUT-HOUSE.

THE world is but an out-house of creation. We have not yet seen the whole. What barns are to mansions, this world is to heaven.

HUMAN LONGING FOR DIVINITY.

ALL humanity, by its very consciousness of weakness, by its very infirmities, by the dim light of its aspirations, longs to find something that is divine.

WHAT IS SACRED?

NOTHING is sacred because it has "come down." It must have an intrinsic sacredness in it which it brings down with itself.

JOYFUL EXPERIENCES.

IF people, instead of seeking joyful experiences for themselves, would make other people's experiences joyful,—would seek to *do* good rather than to *be* good, they would accomplish both objects.

DELICACY.

DELICACY is a spring which God has sunk in the rock, which sends its quiet waters with music down the flowery hillside, and which is pure and transparent, because it has at the bottom no sediment.

MAN'S CHIEF END.

"THE chief end of man is to glorify God,"—not by worshiping him as Oriental men worship princes, for their gorgeousness, but by transmuting our animal and carnal lives into a superb life of service, such as God's is, and by which he is, worthily, the head of all things.

SCIENCE AND RELIGION.

SCIENCE and religion will come together coyly at first like other lovers, but there will be the kiss and embrace, and at last they will marry and there will be no more trouble between them than is usually found in well-regulated families.

THE BIBLE AND SECULAR KNOWLEDGE.

I DO not believe that anything will destroy the hold of the Bible upon men's love and trust. It may be done, however, by claiming for it, what it does not claim for itself—that it is the sum of all secular knowledge.

SELF-RELIANCE.

THE child that is lugged through life on the back of his parent is no better than an Indian papoose. He is nothing but an everlasting baby.

MORAL STATISTICS.

I WOULD to God that there were moral as there are physical statistics. If there were, it would be shown that integrity and permanent prosperity go together.

HOW MEN UNFOLD.

MEN unfold according to their nature. A man of phlegmatic temperament eats slowly, drinks, walks, works, sleeps slowly; and his graces will grow slowly. If a man be quick and nervous, the analogy will run in religion as in everything else. But the principle is, first the blade, then the ear, then the ripe kernel in the ear.

INDIFFERENCE.

INDIFFERENCE is more fatal than skepticism. There is no pulse in indifference. Skepticism may have warm blood; but simple indifference is dead, and therefore fatal.

GENIUS IMMORTAL.

GENIUS is immortal. Like stars, it is not darkened by use, nor extinguished by time. The stars which shone over Eden hang over our dwellings yet; and the works of genius, as far back as there is any record of them, are just as fresh and just as bright at this time as they were at the beginning.

VALUE OF STOCK.

I SUPPOSE there is a great deal in stock. I suppose that some men are born honest men. You would have to begin and untwist the skein to the original tow before you could weaken their honesty.

SERMON ON THE MOUNT.

NO one can take the Sermon on the Mount and apply it to his daily life and not find that he is in an academy which drills him on the right and on the left, and whets and sharpens him.

THE GOLDEN GATE OF DEATH.

WHEN we comprehend the fullness of what death will do for us, in outlook and forelook, dying is triumphing. Nowhere is there so fair a sight, so sweet a prospect, as when a young soul is passing away out of life and time through the gate of death,—the rosy, the royal, the golden, the pearly gate of death.

BRINGING UP BY HEART.

A MOTHER and a dog are the only two things in the world that seem to have absolutely disinterested love.

A mother's heart does more in the bringing up of children, a million times, than a mother's hand, though the hand is sometimes quite busy.

EXPRESSED AFFECTION.

I think love grows between husband and wife by expression of affection. I know there is a stately dignity in vogue. Husband and wife sit over against each other like those great statues of Memnon in Egypt; there they are, vast, stony and hard.

ABRAHAM LINCOLN.

ABRAHAM LINCOLN—a name spoken in every corner of Christendom and added to the roll of those upon whom Time has no power.

REMARKS ABOUT PUBLIC MEN.

ROBERT BURNS—A true poet, made not by the schools, brought up with no external culture or assistance. He came as a flower comes in spring. We say that he was a man of the people. No; he was far above the people. He was ordained to be an interpreter of God to his kind, then and forevermore.

Of all the American novelists who have passed away, the author of "The House of the Seven Gables" seems to be the greatest.

Grant had the patience of Fate and the force of Thor. He has left to memory only such weaknesses as connect him with humanity and such virtues as will rank him among heroes.

John Brown's name will travel through the ages as an illustrious example of what a man may do who is willing to suffer for a great principle.

Emerson, the calm, the observational, not an enthusiast in religion, but with patriotism and humanity to make him a brave witness. It took seven generations of ministers to make one Ralph Waldo Emerson.

It is a noble thing to see a man so in sympathy with his time and work, as Tennyson is, that even with expiring strength he still tries to chant the truth of God to the age in which he lives.

Peter Cooper—a manly man, who lived for his fellow-men. May God increase the procession of such men! He will increase it. It is a tendency.

Though slow, Abraham Lincoln was sure. A

thousand men could not make him plant his foot before he was ready; ten thousand could not move it after he had set it down.

HOW TO KEEP SUNDAY.

THE object of Sunday is to say to that in men which is secular and animal, "Rest;" and to that which is intellectual, moral and social, "Grow!" The prevalent idea of keeping the Sabbath is that it is a day on which certain things must not be done. To the majority of people, Sunday is a day full of *nots*. The week is a house, and Sunday is the best room in it, and should have the best things put into it.

Sunday is not a day designed to enable the church to get a hitch on folks. It is the common people's great liberty-day, and they are bound to see that work does not come into it. I esteem the awfulness that is attached to Sunday, and church, and pulpit, the greatest mistake of Christendom. Sunday is the common people's Magna Charta.

INDUSTRY AND HAPPINESS.

THE poor man with industry is happier than the rich man in idleness. The slave is often happier than the master, who is nearer undone by license than his vassal by toil.

LOOK AT THE FUTURE.

TAKE somebody who is rather faulty, who you think is a slippery Christian, and whom you like to dissect, and remember that the work of grace has begun in him, and lift him up, and imagine what he will be in the future, till you see him enveloped in a flood of God's glory, and then look at him.

NOT IN STRAIGHT LINES.

THE world has never advanced in straight lines, but by spiral—going back on itself as it were, but still advancing on the whole.

GOD'S KINGDOM.

ALL those who have their nobler nature developed until they feel in themselves the inspiration of God's presence, are inhabitants of His kingdom and none others are.

CRADLE AND THRONE.

THE power of the cradle is greater than the power of the throne. Make me the monarch of the cradles, and I will give to whomsoever will the monarchy of kingdoms.

CONCERT PITCH.

DID you ever hear how the string of a harp or a violin complains when you begin to turn the key, and screw up to concert pitch? How it wails! And yet when it is screwed tight, it discourses glorious music—and only then. Men do not liked to be screwed up, but they all want good music brought out of them. God knows better than they do what conditions are required for such music, and he turns the key of life, and brings them, at last, into concord; but it is late before many of them are fit to be played upon.

REPENTANCE.

WHAT repentance is ever logical? Will a shepherd refuse a returned sheep because it followed home a bell-wether instead of the shepherd's own call?"

ORATORS AND FARMERS.

THERE are more passable orators born every year than they are first-class farmers. If any one doubts the truth of this, let him try a farm for a few years.

BORROWING TROUBLE.

I THINK the most humiliating thing a person could do—but our vanity will not let us do it—would be to sit down and think how he has fretted and stewed and simmered in advance, about griefs and troubles which never came as he anticipated they would.

CLEAR HEADS.

I HAVE noticed that God's providence is on the side of clear heads.

CITIZENSHIP.

THE men who cannot be made to be citizens have not the rights of citizens. Rights develop with the advance of moral excellence.

ESCAPING TROUBLE.

THERE are many men that will not get away from trouble when they can. If there is trouble in one room they will not so much as go into another room to avoid it. A wise man, when he finds himself in a room where there is trouble, goes out of it as soon as possible. Now God put at least thirty rooms in a man's mind, and if there is trouble in one, he can go up to the next one, and if the trouble comes into that, he can go up to the next, and, if necessary, he can keep going up-stairs till he gets upon the roof; and the higher he goes, the more tired will troubles get of flying up after him.

IMAGINATION.

BY the light of imagination the noblest geniuses, with the purest of lives are representing something vastly above any average of human experience.

A SHADOW.

I WOULD rather be a nobody, and have no character and no responsibility, than to be one of those miserable, truckling men in God's service, who forever are watching their influence, for fear they shall lose it. Suppose you should see a man going up and down some street, and you should ask him why he did it, and he should say: "God has committed to me the responsibility of a shadow, and I am taking care that I do not lose my shadow!"

WEALTH, A PUNCTUATION.

IT is a pity to see a great dwelling in which everything appears to dwarf the occupant— in which the occupant is but the punctuation of his wealth.

AUTUMN.

AS in Spring all things are coming, so in Autumn all things are going; but not to annihilation. They will rest, but they will rise again.

THE GLOBE A CRADLE.

I THINK that the whole round globe is but a cradle, and that God rocks it with His foot.

REMEMBERING THE PAST.

NEVER remember the past to renew your grief, but only to renew your courage.

CONVERSION.

CONVERSION is to a man's soul just what ripening is to grapes. They hang in the right form; every one of them has skin and seeds; but all of them are sour. But just let them hang there long enough in the bright sunshine till it makes them sweet, and they are converted. That is exactly what conversion means to man. He hangs there, but sour, until he sees what is the power of God, the love of God and the spirit of God becomes sweetened to him.

PRAYER.

IT is the soul that prays first; the tongue wags afterwards. It is no small privilege that we have of talking with God and of laying our troubles upon Him.

LYING.

I DO not think there is a thing about which men sin more than they do in this matter of lying. They lie from their birth. From the womb they go spreading lies. David said, in his haste, that all men were liars; and an old Scotch preacher very shrewdly remarked that he never took it back when he got leisure.

APPLES WITH THE PEEL ON.

THERE are some persons that love apples, who cannot bear to eat them with the peel on; and there are a great many Christians that love to engage in religious devotions who cannot bear go to a prayer meeting.

GOD'S WORK IN NATURE.

MEN cannot do anything in marble, or on canvas, and not have their name pronounced for two hundred years by the shadow of what they have done, so that the world knows them by associating them with their works. But God, for six thousand years, has carved and painted as no man ever carved and painted and we continually behold His works, and who says, "God?" Morning, and noon, and evening come and go, and how many of us say, "God?" All the day long the sun pours down its life-giving rays, and we think of nothing but "Umbrella," or "Harvest," or something of that sort.

HEIRS OF GOD.

GOD says, "I will give you if you ask, myself and all that I have, and make you my heirs;" and when a man is an heir of God, there is a good property coming to him.

POETRY.

THE finest gossamer thread that poetry ever spun has utility as really as the threads which the loom weaves into cloth for bodily wear, and in a far finer and nobler sense.

AMUSING SINS.

IT makes a great difference whether a sin is amusing or not about its being tolerated—laughable lies and wickednesses go along smoothly, when everybody kicks the sober ones.

A MISER'S MAXIM.

MERCY and sympathy are vagrant fowls; and that they may not scale the fence between a man and his neighbor, their wings are clipped by the miser's master-maxim, "*Charity begins at home.*"

TOAD MEN.

GEOLOGISTS sometimes find toads sealed up in rocks. They crept in during the formation periods, and deposits closed the orifice through which they entered. There they remain, in long darkness and toad stupidity, till some chance blast or stroke sets them free. And there are many rich men sealed up in mountains of gold the same way. If, in the midst of some convulsion in the community, one of these mountains is overturned, something crawls out into life which is called a man.

GOD'S HIGHWAY.

WE know what direction in which we are to grow, and what are the materials out of which our growth must come. "Thou shalt love the Lord thy God with all thy heart, and mind and soul, and strength, and thy neighbor as thyself." Here is God's highway. We have got on the turnpike road.

THE ENGINE OF SYMPATHY.

YOU that are strong are to help that man who cannot control his temper; his skin and your skin may be different; it may be that you are made tough, while he is made very tender. If he does not know how to hold himself, do you help him to hold himself; if he cannot extinguish the conflagration that tends to break out, do you bring the engine of your sympathy and help him to put out the fire.

TRYING ON THE SERMON.

IT will not be long after you return to your own household before something will go wrong, and you will get hold of the wrong handle. Then will be your time to say, "Let me try on the sermon." Do try it on. Try it a month—that is not long to wear a garment—and see if it is not the truth that I have been telling you.

IT STICKS TO HIM.

I AM often in a strait, betwixt two. I do believe in conversion, and in the power of new spiritual life; but after all, my own observation has gone to show that a naturally mean man is apt to have his meanness stick to him after he becomes a professor of religion.

FRENCH LITERATURE.

I THINK the ten plagues of Egypt one after another, frogs, lice and all, would not be worse, than is that plague, that intolerable nuisance of French literature. I had rather my child (and I speak the words of truth and soberness) would take his chance in making a journey through pest hospitals, plague hospitals, yellow fever hospitals, five or six of them in succession, than to walk through those pest volumes of even one writer—Eugene Sue.

PERSONAL INFLUENCE.

YOU are not doing half so much as you ought to be doing; you are doing a thousand times more than you dream of.

SOUL FEEDING.

THE mother is not more admirably formed to nourish the infant body by her own, than to nourish its heart by her heart. Its soul feeds at her heart, as much as its body at her bosom, and with this difference, that the child is never weaned from its soul-breast.

PROPHECIES.

PROPHECIES, as I understand them, are things of the vaguest and most general character possible. They are what music is to an army while marching. When Napoleon was going over the Alps, and his soldiers had become nearly exhausted with dragging the heavy artillery after them, he ordered his band to sound a charge, and the moment the soldiers heard that charge, they were indued with double strength, and they pitched up the heights with comparative ease.

LEAN RELIGION.

RELIGION is a very slim, lean, gaunt, poor, ill-fed thing as it is ordinarily conceived of in this world.

WORKING UP TROUBLE.

WORK your troubles up! If a man fills my house with thorns, I will not go about saying, "What a distressed state of things is this!" They are good to make the pot boil, if for nothing else.

SLEAZY MEN.

THERE are some men that are born so sleazy that it seems as though no sewing would make them into garments of any account.

NOT BUILT ALIKE.

SHALL I despise your yacht because it is not built like mine? Yet people insist that in theology we shall be built as much alike as the Newfoundland fishermen are—and as much in the fog, too!

BEST APPLES ON TOP.

WE are apt to carry ourselves as men arrange their stores. The newest and most attractive goods are in the windows; but those which are old, or shop-worn, or rotton, or adulterated, are taken far back in the half-lights, where sharp-eyed clerks sell to bat-eyed customers.

BOOKS.

THANK God for books! And yet thank God that the great realm of truth lies yet outside of books, too vast to be mastered by types or imprisoned in libraries.

NATURAL LAWS.

NATURAL laws are like our post-offices, only they never advertise. If any man has a letter there, he can get it by asking.

JONATHAN EDWARDS.

WHEN Jonathan Edwards, the brightest lamp of centuries on these shores, stood forth, ten thousand bats flew round him, and myriads of moths and millers tried to put out his light, and he was regarded as a great innovator; but in our time there is no lack of men who worship Jonathan Edwards. And, strange to say, the very men who worship these bright examples of Christian heroism, take their old bones, as Samson took the jaw bone of an ass, and stand in the way of the truths which they sought to establish.

CONSCIENCE OUT OF TUNE.

SOME men keep their goodness as people do their pianos. They have them shut up, most of the time, at one side of the parlor; and when they have looked after the affairs of the kitchen, and taken their meals, and waited upon their company, and attended to all their other duties, then, for relaxation, they open them, and play a few tunes upon them. Some men keep their conscience shut up a good part of the time, and once in awhile, for a change, they open it, and play upon it. They find it a little out of tune, but they do not mind that.

A VEGETABLE SOUL.

WE love to fancy that a flower is the point of transition at which a material thing touches the immaterial. It is the sentient vegetable soul.

STRONG REGIMENTS.

IT was a remarkable saying for one of the Revolutionary heroes—when Congress, instead of passing a bill for more soldiers, recommended a day for fasting and prayer—that there might be a good deal in fasting and prayer, but he had noticed that God's providence was on the side of strong regiments.

CRACKED BELLS.

YOU would think to look at that bell up in the belfry, "Oh, such a bell, lifted up so high, it only needs that some one should pull the rope to make it sound gloriously through the air!" Well, pull the rope; it sounds for all the world like a tin pan! It is cracked. I see men in the old belfry of prosperity; and other men are looking up at them and saying, "Oh, how happy they must be!" Well, ring them, and see how they sound.

GOD'S FLOWER BED.

GOD'S flower-bed is oftentimes your sick bed. Joy, patience, and faith that looks beyond the visible, are better than any outward achievement.

GOD'S PROVIDENCE.

I DO not need a God, whose business it is to rub up the stars and keep them bright, to turn the vast wheel of the universe, and by infinite forces to take care of globes and human beings, but a God who tells me, "The hairs of your head are all numbered," and who says, "Not a sparrow falls to the ground without my notice."

GROWLERS.

I OFTEN see men who seem to think that it is a very great thing to squeak at every joint, and that every revolution of business should be accompanied with groans.

APPREHENSION.

TO the blind man the whole world is obliterated. To the deaf man there is no sound in the air by day or by night. All things are dead where there is no spiritual apprehension.

HASTY JUDGMENT.

WITH many men the question is not whether they can be overcome, but at what pressure they can be overcome. All pieces of timber may be broken. Some will bear a ton, some ten tons, some a hundred tons, and some a thousand tons, but there is a point at which the strongest piece of timber will break. And we must not be in a hurry, when a man falls, to say, "'That man was a corrupt old hypocrite."

ELECTION.

DO I believe in the doctrine of election? Certainly. I believe that some men are elected to be mathematicians, and some I *know* are not.

NEEDLESS PRAYERS.

WHAT do angels do with unnecessary anxieties? What clouds of needless prayers are daily floated upward which never distill into rain!

EYE PICTURES.

"MEN'S eyes make finer pictures when they know how to use them, than anybody's hands can."

ASPIRATION.

THE very willingness of men to try new views of new ways springs from the developed desire for the renovation of human nature.

CHILDREN LIKE ANIMALS.

CHILDREN at first are mere animals. The most absolute animals on the globe, I think are these little pulpy children. They are, as they roll about, like sunfish floating through the water—round, plump, and beautiful to look at, but good for nothing—absolutely nothing. I will not say they are at zero—they are below zero. They seem to be the connecting link between nothing and something, and very faintly revealed at that.

SELF-INCLOSURE.

WE are not obliged to sit in our minds with all the doors open, nor with all the windows open. We have a right of reserve, of self-inclosure, of refusing to let men know what we are, what we think, and what we do.

WEALTH AND MANHOOD.

I SAY that that idea of manhood which makes one man high because he is pocket-ful, and another man low because he is pocket-empty, is heathenish, and unworthy of men who have lived any length of time within sight of a Bible.

TO-DAY'S DUTY.

NOW God says "Here is your duty for to-day, and the means with which to do it. To-morrow you will find remittances and further directions; next week you will find other remittances and other directions; next month you will find others; and next year still others."

PUBLIC SENTIMENT.

COULD the public sentiment declare that *personal morality* is the first element of patriotism, that corrupt legislators are the most pernicious of criminals, that the judge who lets the villain off is the villain's patron, that tolerance of crime is intolerance of virtue, our nation might defy all enemies and live forever.

TRASHY RELIGION.

I THINK that of all the trashy things in this world, the most trashy are a religion that don't do anything, and flowery sermons, and gingerbread books, that begin in the mouth and end in the ear.

HOW TO VOTE.

NO man has a right to go to the polls who does not go with the determination to have his own way if he can, and to let other people have theirs if he cannot, and to accept the situation when it has been fairly decided by the ballot.

LIBERTY OF THOUGHT.

YOU cannot give liberty of thought and action to men without producing beneficent results. Its product has been the same wherever it has been enjoyed.

LIKE A MUSKET.

MEN come at last to that state in which wrong-doing is like one of Queen Anne's muskets, that kills at the muzzle and kicks at the breech.

LESSONS FROM ROCKS.

WHENEVER you see a man laugh, laugh with him; whenever you see a man glad, you be glad, too. The rocks could tell you that. If one of a joyous company, in some valley, beneath an overhanging cliff, breaks out into a merry, ringing laugh, all the rocks laugh back again.

VALUE OF MORAL INFLUENCE.

A MAN has fifty thousand dollars to invest. Where does he invest it? Does he take up land or stocks in a village that never hears the church bell ring? No; he says, "If I should go to such a place, my property would never increase; it would never pay any dividend; it would be a dead weight on my hands." A man wishes to invest his money where there are the most active men, and where there is the most moral influence. The place where there is the most true Christianity, is the place to invest money.

WHAT MEN LACK.

THE great trouble with man is not a lack of opportunity, it is the need of a disposition to improve the opportunities they have.

FALSE ACCUSATIONS.

A TEN-THOUSANDTH part of the things alleged against a man that are alleged against the Eternal Creator, would drive him out of society.

SINGING VIRTUES.

NO man has a right to put himself in a crystal case, and have his virtues sing to him like so many canary birds.

BURY YOUR SINS.

DO not make your sins like an Egyptian mummy, with its dried bones and muscles wrapped up in gummed hideousness. Let your past sins be buried, and if you want to go to the graveyard once in a while to see where you have laid them, go, but don't bring home anything with you.

THE SECRET OF LIFE.

THIS, then, is the secret of life—to seek all you can lay your hand on, but to seek it only as a round of a ladder which is good for nothing for a man to sit and roost on, but is good to enable him to take another step being only preliminary to the next.

APPETITES NOT SINFUL.

THE doctrine of sin is one of the fundamental doctrines of any system of theology; and that doctrine lies very near to a high state of regenerative religion; but the form and color derived from that form of teaching which came from the mediæval scholastic theology has given to sin a false place, and to its philosophy falsehood. We are emerging from the pessimist view of the mind of man, and of the nature of his passions, of his appetites, of his body, and are coming to believe that they are all factors that lead to sin, but that they are not in and of themselves sinful. The functions of the earlier periods of human development are relatively imperfect, but they are indispensable. A child cannot grow up into manhood without passing through all the intermediary stages. You cannot break ground with a bean, and at the same instant have it fifteen feet high, twining around a pole, and bearing blossoms and pods. It must go up by regular stages, little by little, through periods of time, and under the ministration of moisture, of heat, and of light; and finally it comes to full growth. So it is the decree of God that men shall come little by little to the unfolding of themselves.

NOT YET RIPE.

AFTER I have blazed out on a man I can generally get up and regret that I did it, and feel sorry for him; but nature is very strong, and the old way of dealing with evil right in the face, blow for blow, is very natural—too natural altogether. The higher way is that by which we medicate evil through compassion, through patience, through gentleness, through self-sacrifice. The using of one's self against men that are evil, not to harm them, but to reform them, and to draw them to a better and a higher life—ah! I would to God that I were a better example to you of that. I would to God that you would try as hard as I do to have that example. I have learned it somewhat, so that if a thing does not come too fast and too hot I generally refuse malign feelings toward those that injure me; but I confess that I am not ripe yet. The sour juice has not yet become quite saccharine enough in me. Nevertheless, I do not exempt myself from duty, and I judge myself, my standing, and the truth and reality of the Christian religion as exemplified by me, and not by my knowledge, and not by my good-natured hours, not by the amount of enjoyment which I take in the æsthetic exercise of worship, and not by conscience even, but by the power that I have of meeting hatred with love, and, more than that, of serving, instead of punishing, those that do me harm.

HUNGER FOR FAME.

OH, that we could remove the curse of the hunger for fame, and give in its place the substantial hunger for real excellence without recognition or reward.

PRIVATE RIGHTS.

THE private rights of a public man should be guarded as sacredly as the altar of a temple. If the President of the United States pursues an inhuman course towards the Indian; if he transgress the canons of liberty which he is sworn to defend; if he wink at evils which he is bound to prevent or suppress, he deserves severe public rebuke. But in his own private home, whether he manages his individual affairs with economy or stinginess, whether he drinks whiskey at his table, or nothing but cold water, whether he dresses well or ill, talks much or little, spends his income in one way or another —these and all such-like things do not belong to him as President, but as a private man, and are sacred from remark. For good morals every man may be held responsible. There ought to be but one key to a man's privacy, and that is in his own hands; but the devil has given everybody a key to it, and everybody goes in and out and filches whatever he pleases.

CHARGING AGAINST A HEART.

NOBODY will tell you some things. Even your pastor won't. I would rather any time go into the battle-field, unskilled as I am in soldiery; I would rather cut off a man's leg, little as I know about surgery, and then take care of him, than to tell a person his faults. I think to charge one of the batteries of Sevastopol was no more than it is to charge right up against a man's heart.

LOOKING HEAVENWARD.

YOU have probably noticed that when men walk across a stream on a timber, if they look at their feet to see where they step, their head begins to swim, and very soon they have to swim or drown; whereas, if they fix their eye upon a single object on the opposite bank, and never look at their feet at all, they reach the other side in safety. Now, if a man stands looking at this world, he gets dizzy and intoxicated, and falls; whereas, if he fixes his eye upon the bank of the eternal world, he walks straighter in this world, and is more sure of reaching the other side in safety.

PRETENDERS TO VIRTUE.

I HAVE seen the heaviest establishments with the simplest sign over the door, while a petty huckster filled his windows with about every article in the shop; and I have seen persons so violently indignant at missteps in others, that I suspected that all the virtue they had was at the window!

ILLUSTRIOUS MARTYRS.

THERE are men that seem to think they would suffer willingly if they were called to suffer as martyrs, illustriously. Ah! that is just the thing. You would be willing to be placed where you would have to suffer, and where you would yet get the credit of suffering. But it is pinching suffering that God calls you to endure. He knows where your weakness requires that you should suffer, and there he makes you suffer. Like a driver, he puts the stroke of the lash in those very places where he knows it will make you wince.

COMFORTERS.

NOW, many men have the office of comforters. It ought to be the office supremely of a physician. No man is fit to be a doctor merely because he knows medicine. No man is a true doctor or physician, though he may be a true surgeon, who does not understand the interior economy of a man—his dispositional as well as his physiological life. Structure and function are not all. Men say that the reason that homœopathy prevails is, that they who practise it play on the imagination. I do not care what they play on, if the outcome is help. I do care, too; for the less I take the better I feel. What if it be imagination? What if a man has such discernment that he can see that if he can lift up a patient's disposition, and therefore lift up his relaxed nerves, it will brace up the whole person, and says, "I will make him cure himself?" Nobody outside of surgery ever does cure anybody: he who gets well always gets well himself; and blessed be the physician that knows how, whether by medicine or by his own personal quality, to persuade men to get well, by giving nature a chance to operate and lift them out of their dismal condition.

RELIGION TRUE.

"OH, religion is true! It is of God. It leads to God." All the outside performances of religion may be invalid, empty, and useless; but wherever the heart is taken possession of by this divinest spirit of gentleness, sympathy, compassion, pity, and love, it reigns on the dark earth as stars on the dark sky of the night.

TALE-BEARING.

A DOCTOR might as well stand with his saddle-bags and scatter their contents through the community as a man tell all he knows about people indiscriminately.

A WELL-BUILT MAN.

SOME men go through life as steamers do through the sea, beating every wave with paddles and bows, determined to domineer over wind and storm. But it must be a well-built man that can put his prow into life, and go in a straight line to the point at which he aims, by means of his own sheer sagacity and strength.

SPIRITUAL EVOLUTION.

WE are all of us merely developing spirit in matter or out of matter. We are gaining that victory which God means the immortal shall gain over the mortal, the transient, the perishing. We are producing from these roots, these stems—our bodies— blossoms and fruits which God shall be willing to pick, that he may show them again in another life.

OPPORTUNITY IN AMERICA.

WE grumble—we inherit that from our ancestors; we often mope and vex ourselves with melancholy prognostications concerning this or that danger. Some men are born to see the devil of melancholy; they would see him sitting in the very door of heaven, methinks. Not I; for though there be mischiefs and troubles, yet when we look at the great conditions of human life in society, and they have been augmented favorably, they never were so favorable as they are to-day. More than that: if you will look at the diversity of the industries by which men ply their hands, if we look at the accumulating power of the average citizen, you will find that it is in the power of a man to earn more in a single ten years of his life to-day than for our ancestors in the whole of their life.

AMERICA'S VITALITY.

THE power of a nation is to be judged by its resistance to disease. All nations are liable to attack, but the real power of a nation is shown in its ability to throw off disease. The power of recovery is better than all soundness of national constitution. It is better than anything else can be. America has arisen from a fifth-rate power; but she looks calmly and modestly over the ocean, and is a first-rate power among the nations to-day. She was a democracy; the people made their own laws; they levied and collected their own taxes; and it was said, "Of course they will not allow themselves to be taxed more than they want to be." We were not a military people; Europe told us so. Great Britain told us so. They told me so to my face; and I said on many a platform, "You do not understand what democratic liberty means. Wait till this game is played out, and see what the issue is." And what is the issue of the game? The genius of the Northern people is slow to get on fire, and is hard to put out; so that we had to learn the trade of war. We had learned every trade of peace already, but when once we had learned the trade of war, the power of the North was manifest, to the honor and glory of our religion, of our political faiths, and of the whole training of our past history.

ROBUST MORALITY.

FOR myself, I know of but one refuge (though to the pure all things are pure), and that is the simple morality of the New Testament—that simple-hearted, robust morality, with an up-and-down love of right, and an up-and-down hatred of wrong.

LIVING IN A CELLAR.

THE man who trusts in God, lives in the upper story of his head; while the man who does not trust in God, lives in the lower story of his head. The man who trusts in God, lives in an observatory, where he enjoys the sunlight and the pure atmosphere of heaven; while the man who does not trust in God, lives down in a dank and dungeon cellar.

EXCUSES FOR LAZINESS.

THERE are educated men in this congregation that have no business to be unoccupied on Sunday. I know what the excesses of labor are; I know how hard the city grinds; I know that there are some men that cannot do this work; but I know that for all of the thousands who resort here Sunday night and morning there cannot be that excuse. There are men who are like trunks packed in a garret—whose heads are never opened from year to year. There are men in this congregation who have the capacity of inspiring enterprise in the young, but who are too selfish. They want to stay at home, or take a ride in Central Park. They cannot give up their afternoon. One is too feeble, one has too much domestic care, one has had his turn (was once a teacher), and so forth. "I pray thee have me excused." They all want to be excused, and sit down on the cushion of self-indulgence, and call themselves Christians.

THE PRESENT AGE.

THERE was never a time, I think, in which it was so well worth a man's while to live. There was never a time when society touched a man on so many sides. At every faculty there is some hand knocking at the door and asking entrance. There never was a time when common people could know as much of history, as much of science, as much of art, as much of administration. In former days a man might say, "I know nothing of all these things; how can I be blamed?" but no man can say that to-day.

HUMOR.

I HAVE noticed in great assemblies that when men get by the ears, and their combative feelings have arisen, and they are ready for a fierce conflict, one good stroke of humor puts it all back, and the men smile, and look at each other with friendly eyes. I tell you, humor is the friend of conscience; and any man whose conscience does not want humor I suspect keeps worse company than that—the company of combativeness and destructiveness.

APPRECIATING GENIUSES.

IT may be said that, so far as history is concerned, there is no conception of God finer than that developed by Moses in the Old Testament. "How is that for evolution?" you will say. I will simply reply, that when Moses lived mankind had been living for a million years on the earth; that there were the materials for the formation of an idea of the divine Being; that though they were sparse, relatively, there were a few lines of light, and that his was one of those appreciating geniuses, like Shakespeare's, which took ten thousand things that had been living around about, and did not invent them, but felt them, and saw them, and drew them into the mightiness of his own soul, so that they became a part of his ocean nature. They had happened before, and many of them were insignificant until he made them stand in the grandeur of his architecture and the beauty of his fabric.

A TRANSITION PERIOD.

THE transition which we are making to-day is out of the mediæval and monarchial construction of human society into an atmosphere fashioned not so much by considerations of the state as by the higher disclosures of men's moral lives, by the sweetness of the family, by the realm of philanthropy, by the dawning and practical enforcing of the idea that the whole human family belong to each other, and that love should be radiant among men. This larger conception of God, which is not yet really fashioned and formed into any definite theology, is struggling for an expression, first negatively, by knocking off the barbarisms that have existed hitherto; and the men that still cling to antiquity are shocked at the idea.

UNCONSCIOUS DISTURBERS.

NOW, a man should study somewhat his own natural carriage. In the household is a man grave, slow, without any blossoming? He is a dullard; he is an ox; yet he may not be within. He lives with one that has flashing nerves, and is as quick as mercury; and against that man he is prejudiced; he is out of patience with him. Is one nervous? Does he feel quickly and express himself quickly? And does he dwell with others that also are sensitive? The very habit of speaking abruptly or decisively hurts, in the family, and elsewhere. The things are unconscious, and all the more because the man who indulges in them may be conscientious, upright, and want to do right. As when, for instance, a great weighty Newfoundland dog rushes into the parlor, treads on the table and upsets the children, he does not mean anything but caress, so there are men that overthrow each other with rude contacts and unconscious violence, disturbing the peace and harmony of all with whom they have to do. There is a good deal of room for people to study themselves in these minor directions; for a man may be just, a truth-speaker, and a conscientious man, and yet be perpetually disturbing the balance of things.

THE WORLD IN A PANIC.

IF in a great crowd assembled on some public occasion there should spring up a panic of alarm, and forthwith every person should commence rushing, dashing, overthrowing the weak, and treading down children, the whole great throng doing mischief upon each other, it would imperfectly represent what is going on all over the world. There is not a house where there are not frictions. There is not a neighborhood where there are not misunderstandings I had almost said, there is not a church where there are not quarrels. From the very fountain of sanctity, wedded love, from that little imperial realm, the household, the empire of affection, we still hear the murmur, the outcry, or sometimes even the passionate voice of discord; and if you go up and down through the community with moral experience and well-adjusted power of analysis and judgment, I think you will find, not that the unhappiness which prevails in the world comes from great strokes of misfortune, though there are many of these, but that the tone of happiness is lowered, and the actual uprising of unhappiness is caused by the carriage of men among themselves. To a very large extent it is the result of little things.

PARTIAL VIEW OF GOD.

WHEN a large landscape is to be taken by photography, it is taken in sections, and then, when struck off, they are put together on a surface, so that the whole can be drawn out. No instrument is large enough to take in a quadrant. So it is with the idea of God in any one individual. It is restrained and measured by the limitation of his own individuality. Some men that have immense sympathy and benevolence see nothing but goodness—goodness not tempered by justice, goodness not as part and parcel of a great administrator. Some men that are intensely conscientious and stern in their sense of justice form an idea of God as an imperial sovereign. To them He is, first, middle, and last, the Sovereign. The doctrine of sovereignty has been one of the most universal over all men in hard times, and men of stern nature have clung to that view of God almost to the losing sight of the other side; whereas, there are many men, artists in nature, to whom God is manifested more through the channels of beauty than through all other channels. If you could enter in and see as they see, you might say: "That may be your God, but I never had such a God before." It is so from the immensity of the divine Being, and from the fact that we fashion the conception of God. For the conception is all that we have. He is invisible, incommunicable. "No man shall see Him and live." I had almost said the meaning of it was that no man shall see Him until he is dead. "We shall see Him as He is," breaks out in another place. "Now, we see as through a glass darkly," says another of the interlocutors of the New Testament. God is so large, so vast, that nobody sees Him. Not only that, it is not to be supposed that any man ever has a comprehension that takes in the whole cycle and circle of the divine existence. We are each of us seeing a little.

A NOBLE LIFE.

A LIFE that is full of brightness; a life that is filled with sweetness; a life that moves as flowers move, borne in your hands, carrying their fragrance with them, and scattering it everywhere; a life patient, gentle, forgiving, knowing no evil, thinking none, believing in none, seeking all that is good, pure, true, and making others happy—oh, what a life is that! and if that life pervaded the whole community, how blessed would be that community! That is the life that you are called to.

SPIRITUAL EDUCATION.

PUT a violin into the hands of a young practitioner (or, for the whole neighborhood, more agreeable, probably, a piano); spread before him the Fifth Symphony of Beethoven, or

Schumann's works. The question is, Ought that child to play these? Certainly he ought; it is his duty to do it, if you give him time and practice enough. Is it his duty to do it to-day, this moment? No; it is impossible for him to do it to-day; but by and by, with suitable influence exerted upon him, and with patience of practice, he will come to them. I say it is possible for a man to play all the way through the Fifth Symphony, but I say it is impossible for him to do it until he studies and is educated to do it.

That which is true of these more familiar instances is true of the whole round of unfolding —that is, of education; for spiritual results come from education as much as these lower and secular forms of development.

Now, say to a man that just comes into a conscious purpose of living a Christ-like life, "You must love your enemies." "Not by a good deal," he says; "I tried it yesterday, and I could not do it; everything was in revolt with me." So it was, and yesterday he could not do it. Was he therefore released from the duty of doing it? No. The pressure of the divine ideal was still upon him. Those words have never been revoked They echo down through the ages to-day. They come to us before we have learned, just as every attainment in lower education comes. You must strive and attain to it.

OBSCURE HEROES.

WHY does a man of honor tell the truth? Because he loves the truth; because anything less is unseemly in his mind, as is a discord to a musician's ear, or a lack of harmony in color on the palette to the painter's eye. In the sight of God deeds are judged by their moral quality, and not by the effects which they are producing upon men, nor by those auxiliaries by which you crutch yourself along in a moral course. For example, a violent passion subdued in the secrecy of one's own chambered will, stands before God for heroism. If one were adapting himself to some great enterprise, or some public trust, or conspicuous place, and should say, "I have a strong temptation for intoxicating drinks, and I must kill that serpent;" or, "I am parsimonious, and that will be against my opportunity, and so I will force myself to give: it will be a good expenditure for ambition;" if a man, in other words, contests the passions of his nature and his character for some exterior reason, for some consideration of profit, I will not say that he should not do it, but I will say that this is the very poorest kind of heroism—so poor that it is out at the elbows. If a man has a lion-like passion, let him, as David did, attack the lion; let him, as the great heroes of antiquity did, go forth to slay the python. A man's mind is to be toward the good, and for the sake of the good he is to confess the evil. Whether any man knows it or not, whether it will make any difference in the market, or in the Court of Trumpets, or not, the right thing is to be done for its own sake. Do you say, "Oh, well, that is fantastic, that is imaginary; nobody does so!" Perhaps nobody does with whom you consort; but there are a good many in this world that do. There are more obscure heroes than visible ones in this world.

REFORM.

REFORM is God's remedy against revolution. If nations will accept the indications of

God's providence, and make gradual changes, they will grow without compressions and explosions; but where they will not, and hidden forces are perpetually drawing up the steam, by and by they will have a worse revolution just because they will not let off the steam by reformation. But after that, what? Better—a great deal better. All Europe is better than it was before the French Revolution. That was an awful volcanic eruption; the ground shook; the very hills spurted lava; but though it looked in those days as if the end had come, how beautiful now it is! and how far advanced democratic France to-day is over the monarchial France of one hundred and fifty years ago! We cannot foresee, we do not know, what is going to happen; but one thing we do know, that God reigns, and that the light of intelligence, of literature, has been so far disclosed that no raven wing can sweep it back again. Once let the sun come over the east, and you cannot stop it; it will ride triumphant through the whole day, shining brighter and brighter to the end. The rising light of knowledge, the rising light of true religion, the rising light of liberty and regenerative manhood, has come, it has come to stay; and the whole earth shall see the salvation of our God.

WATER-LOGGED SAINTS.

IT is a man dying with his harness on that angels love to take. I hope those old water-logged saints that died soaking in damp stone cells were taken to Heaven. They had hell enough on earth, and it would be a pity for them to have a continuation of it in the other world; but I think they were the poorest of all human commodities ever taken in!

THE WORLD'S ADVANCE.

THERE was not a house in all Athens that you would put your dog into and call it a decent kennel. The Athenians lived in houses that protected them from the sun and rain, and that was all. They had no carpets, no costly furniture, no pictures, no embellishments. Art was consecrated to the State and to religion. In Athens there were no newspapers, no magazines, no libraries. There was no home circle. The wife was a drudge whose only duty was to take care of slaves. She could not unveil her face in the presence of men, nor could she even come to the door to greet her husband or her sons when they came back from battle. Though the lofty mount of the Acropolis gleamed with marble temples, the sun each day finding and leaving it the most resplendent point on the globe, yet at the bottom it was villainously stenchful; and the condition of its inhabitants was mean in comparison with that of the poorest laborer in our time.

NEED OF RULES.

MEN need rules before they have principles; but rules should lead to principles; and principles to intuition.

THEY DESERVE PITY.

WHEN I find persons with nothing to do in life, persons who are educated, of great resources, of great imagination, of great affection, great thinking powers, very active, but nothing to do; too rich to be obliged to work, and placed in a high position in society—(there is nothing worse)—staying at home, reading a great deal, thinking a great deal, rolling and rolling over feelings a great deal—when such persons come to me, my first thought is, God help them! If the Lord in His good providence would only send some dispensation to take away their property, so they would be forced to work, so they would have to go out to work as the servant girls do, go out and wash for a living, most of them would be very happy saints before they had washed a year.

RIGHT USE OF THE WORLD.

A GREAT many men are addicted to much lugubrious soliloquizing and complaining about this unsatisfying world; but whether it is satisfying or not depends upon what men try to satisfy themselves with. If a man were to take a watch and try to use it as a compass, to steer a ship by, he would say: "How unsatisfying this watch is!"

THE WORSE THE BETTER.

NOW, when you wish to please God, treat Him as one who feels sorry for sinners; treat Him as one who longs to help those that need help; go to Him confidingly. No matter how bad you are—the worse the better. Old Martin Luther said, "I bless God for my sins." He would never have had such a sense of the pardoning mercy of God, if he had not himself been sinful.

A CIVILIZING GOSPEL.

THERE are multitudes of mechanics who to-day have more comforts than were in palaces in the time of Queen Elizabeth. If you call to mind the way in which barons used to spread their tables and spend their lives, you will find that the day laborer of our time is better off than they were. The household has augmented itself since then. It requires more to make a good father and a good husband now than it did then. Men are so much larger now, in this country, that an American household today is an institution to compare with which, a hundred or two hundred, a thousand or two thousand, years ago, there was nothing; and the foundations of it are not shaken. Some folks think when the night cart rolls by and shakes the house, that there is an earthquake. No; and mud carts may run by the family, and shake it a little, but there is no earthquake. The social power in the family ministered by the affections, by refined taste, by ardent loves, by joys which have their pattern and equal nowhere else—it is this that marks the civilizing and Christianizing influence of the Gospel in our day.

LOVE, GOD'S VICEGERENT.

LOVE sits as God's vicegerent in the soul, and I will not fight with my brethren. There is now and then a man who is not susceptible to love, or anything else that is good, and I deem it necessary to exterminate vermin wherever they may be found; but I will love all my brethren if they will let me.

HYMNS.

HYMNS are like trumpet calls to a sleeping warrior, which wake him and instantly bring him to his feet, sword in hand.

AN EXCUSE FOR INFIDELITY.

WHEN ministers, and elders, and members of the church, instead of loving each other, are seen wrangling, and quarreling, and railing at one another; when they exhibit natures as full of selfish passions as a sepulchre is of dust and vermin, it is not to be wondered at that scepticism and infidelity are rife among us.

A RELIGION OF VARNISH.

THAT miserable varnish which men stick on the outside, and call it religion; that miserable estimate which they make of religion, that chattering of prayers, that face-religion, that Sunday-keeping religion; all that so-called religion which is but an external covering of pride and selfishness, of worldliness and vanity—the curse and wrath of God abideth upon it. Nowhere else are there such terrific anathemas against such religion as those which fell from the lips of Christ Jesus. It is enough to make a man tremble, to give a man the chills and fever, to walk through those chapters in the Bible where Christ preached to Tract Society men.

USELESS PREACHING.

THE preaching of many men is like children creeping in the sand. Their sermons contain pretty things, perhaps, sweet sentences, but they make no impression upon the hearer. There are fifty-two Sabbaths in the year, and the order of the church has been that there shall be two sermons preached each Sabbath—one in the morning, and one in the afternoon—no matter whether a man wants to preach them or not.

Many men preach twice each Sunday for this reason, and no other. If asked, "What do you preach for?" they say, "Because I must." "Why must you?" "Because I am expected to." They do not preach because there are prevailing errors to be overthrown; not because there are buddings of desire to be expanded into blossoms; not because of any sympathy they feel for the erring and the lost; nor because they feel, "Woe is me if I preach not the Gospel;" but they preach because it is Sunday, and they have got to When Sunday comes round, such a preacher says to himself, "What under the sun shall I preach about?" and the people, when they have heard him, say, "What under the sun did he preach about?"

HOW CHILDREN UNFOLD.

OUR children unfold slowly and the lowest faculties develop first. After the animal nature has got a start then the portion in which the affections reside, grows next; that part which opens the understanding, grows next; and that part which assimilates the child to spiritual beings, grows last. There is some comfort in this, when you see how like little witches your children act sometimes. You think they are certainly bound for the jail or the gallows, until there comes to be an equilibration between the moral feelings and the lower propensities.

WISHING.

A GREAT many people think that a wish is a resolution, but it's gone into proverb that "if wishes were horses, then beggars might ride." A man wishes he was rich; but he's too lazy, he never will be. A man wishes he knew more; probably never will. He's lazy. A man wishes he could have influence in the circles in which society moves, but he stops. He will never have wisdom and patience to do it. And so men stand over against the great objects in life. Men should be respected, but they are not respected. They wish for that which will endure. That would be a purpose. They wish the thing without taking the intermediate step. So men are fools all over the world. Wishing, wishing, wishing. They must be fools when they believe that wishing is some sort of resolution toward competency.

RESOLUTION.

RESOLUTION means a purpose, a will itself. And it includes in it all the intermediate and indispensable intermediate steps. Some resolutions execute themselves immediately, some with some delay, some with long delay, some with many subordinate resolutions that carry out the primary one, and a man may resolve at a critical moment that which will determine the whole career of his life; yea, and determine in any one single final moment that which will take the whole of his life to carry into effect. When my father was yet a lad (he was brought up substantially by an uncle) he had in him all that was necessary to make him what he was in his professional life, but he didn't know it. He was careless, he was heedless, he was very good externally, and so his uncle, going out one morning, found that he was out late with the horse the night before visiting some young companion. The bridle was thrown there on the barn floor, and the horse turned in without a halter. He said: "Oh, well, Lyman will never make a farmer;" and so, talking in the orchard with him one day, he says: "Lyman, how would you like to go to college?" No answer. They went on working all day. The next day, about the same hour, as they worked together in the orchard, Lyman said: "I should like to go, sir." That settled it. And in that liking to go there was a purpose that shaped differently his whole life. It never gave out; it branched in every direction, bore fruit, and finally made him what he was. That was the starting point. He made a tolerably good minister and a tolerably good father.

VALUE OF SUFFERING.

THE greatest achievements of life have been made by those that were sufferers. When the Huguenots, the Vaudois, and the various European nations that suffered under persecutions in the wilderness, in the mountains, and in caves, were driven out, they were unknown, they were of little influence, they were the poor of the earth, they were looked down upon by princes, by priests, and by arch-priests, they were regarded as rubbish; for their faith's sake they suffered loss of property, loss of home, loss of their own kindred, and were subjected to every strait and stress of affliction, and they became heroes; and to-day our children read their history; they are living still; and with an invisible influence they are lifting up men's thoughts to higher spheres and to nobler patience and endeavor. If you go back to the names that are still above the horizon, there is scarcely one of them that has not had this elevation by reason of his conduct as a sufferer.

POORLY FURNISHED WITHIN.

ONE may be free from all vices and from great sins, and yet break God's whole law. That law is love. Many say to themselves, "What wrong do I do?" The question is, What right do you do? An empty grape-vine might say, "Why, what harm do I do?" Yes, but what clusters do you produce? Vitality should be fruitful. Men are content if they can eat, and drink, and be clothed, and keep warm, and go on thus from year to year; because they say, " I cheat no one, I do not lie or steal, nor am I drunk. I pay my debts, and what lack I yet?" A man that can only do that is very poorly furnished within. And in no land in the world are men so culpable who stand still as in this land of Christian light and privileges.

SLANDER.

YOU cannot indulge in badinage, you cannot retail all manner of stories, and not hurt and wound somebody. It is a shame that you, who profess to suffer like the Master rather than create suffering, should go about, wholesale and retail, with all manner of devil's stories. You think these are peccadilloes. Yes, they are just the kind of peccadilloes that carry men to hell!

Do not listen to these things. You would not allow any person to come into your house and sit down with your children and yourself and tell slanderous stories. You would not permit to be read at your fireside, with your innocent daughters listening around, many of the vile scandals that are published. You would oust the man that should attempt to read them there, and would burn the paper that contained them.

You ought not to permit anybody to violate this law of peace, purity, love, and kindness in your presence. If men would refuse to hear these things, and would rebuke them by their silence and their attitude, there would be much fewer tale-bearers.

WHOLESOME MIRTH.

EVERY man ought to have more imagination every year than he has had; that is, it ought to be fed, made sensitive, made useful. Every man that has given to him the gift of wit and humor, instead of letting that spring run out and run dry because he is a Christian, should not so totally misapprehend it. In this world where there is so much drudgery, where there are so many tears and so many clouds, blessed is he that knows how to put a rainbow on the clouds. Blessed is that man who knows how to make his hours cheerful. Of all things that tend to expel the curmudgeons of care, and the mean devils that afflict men, I do not know of any like wholesome mirth. I know that it is not puritanical. The Puritans had another thing to attend to. That was not their particular calling. Since by reaction this had been dissipated and carried to an undue extent, and to impure methods, they rebounded from it. But I look upon the higher qualities of hopefulness, mirthfulness, humor, all good-fellowship, as being of transcendent value in the Christian life.

RIGHT TOWARD THE GOSPEL.

SOME men are preaching, in their rawest way, the old doctrines of punishment. Multitudes of men are preaching the doctrine of a future retribution in those forms and similitudes and figures that were necessary to wake up the low and animal appetites of men Many a man is preaching to men as if they were asses, oxen, wild steeds to be managed by whip, spur, harness or what not. Over against them come the men of sentiment and poetry, who denounce this stormy preaching of hell and damnation, and preach of things airy and beautiful and weak. Then there is the rigorous orthodox, who derides the sentimentalists; and the sentimentalists want nothing to do with the vulgar orthodox. So there is a territory between the upper and the lower that is not yet well defined, nor at all well understood. The Christian moral consciousness revolts against the old material, barbaric, dramatic representations of terror-inspiring fear; and folks think it is going away from the Gospel. I say it is going right toward the Gospel. It is thought to be a decadence of power. It is the luminousness of a higher power. It changes the method of address; and revivalists find that their instruments are dropping out of their hands; but if they only knew it, there are better instruments for their use.

YOUNG LOVE.

ALL strong emotion is evanescent; and if it cannot commute itself into some permanent form it speedily runs out. In the beginning love —the largest, the most effluent, the noblest of all the mind's emotions—rises and flames and pours itself abroad. Then it is that men see angels. Then it is that man feels ecstasies. But the years flow on, with cares, and sorrows, and multiplied labor and infirmity; and the old husband looks into the homely brown face of the wife, and is there any great lifting up of the horizon? Not at all. Then has love been strangled by duty? Is there none? There never was so much; but it has been commuted. It has changed from an emotion into an action, into a habit, into a will-power.

Talk about young love! One could desire to be young again, unless he had loved when he was old, for the brightness and the beauty of the early feeling; but ah! there is no such depth, no such width, no such treasure, as in those later years, when every thought, every feeling springs out of that latent love quality, which, uniting men once, unites them forever and forever.